WHAT DO YOU SEEK?

WHAT DO YOU SEEK?

*The Questions of Jesus
as Challenge and Promise*

Michael J. Buckley, SJ

WILLIAM B. EERDMANS PUBLISHING COMPANY
GRAND RAPIDS, MICHIGAN

Wm. B. Eerdmans Publishing Co.
2140 Oak Industrial Drive N.E., Grand Rapids, Michigan 49505
www.eerdmans.com

2021-01

ISBN 978-0-8028-7395-8

22 21 20 19 18 17   2 3 4 5 6 7

Library of Congress Cataloging-in-Publication Data

Names: Buckley, Michael J., author.
Title: What do you seek? : the questions of Jesus
as challenge and promise / Michael J. Buckley, SJ.
Description: Grand Rapids, Michigan : Eerdmans Publishing Company, 2016. |
Includes bibliographical references and index.
Identifiers: LCCN 2016016407 | ISBN 9780802873958 (pbk. : alk. paper)
Subjects: LCSH: Jesus Christ—Teachings—Miscellanea. | Questioning.
Classification: LCC BS2415 .B728 2016 | DDC 232.9/54—dc23
LC record available at https://lccn.loc.gov/2016016407

To Mary and Jim
with gratitude and admiration

CONTENTS

FOREWORD

Michael J. Buckley, SJ, is a Jesuit whose legacy in philosophical theology, the history of ideas, Ignatian spirituality, and Jesuit education is well established. A great deal of his scholarly life has been spent investigating the nature of belief and unbelief, the mutually beneficial relations of science and religion, the history and theological dynamics of Ignatian spirituality, and the distinctive goals and responsibilities of Catholic higher education.

Fr. Buckley is especially known among scholars for his magisterial study *At the Origins of Modern Atheism* (Yale, 1987). This work was preceded by *Motion and Motion's God: Thematic Variations in Aristotle, Cicero, Newton and Hegel* (Princeton, 1971), and followed by *Denying and Disclosing God: The Ambiguous Progress of Modern Atheism* (Yale, 2000). These works complement treatments of explicitly Catholic and ecclesial themes as displayed in his *Papal Primacy and the Episcopate: Towards a Relational Understanding* (Herder, 1998), and the fruit of years of work in educational history and theory in *The Catholic University as Promise and Project: Reflections in a Jesuit Idiom* (Georgetown, 1998).

These scholarly accomplishments led to his appointment to the faculty of the Gregorian University in Rome and the Jesuit School of Theology in Berkeley, and subsequently to endowed chairs at the University of Notre Dame, Boston College, and Santa Clara University. He was also named a lifetime fellow of Clare College, Cambridge. Additionally, he held institutional commitments beyond the academy that included his service as the chair of the Jesuit International Theological Commission, the president of the Catholic Theological Society of America, and the executive director of the Committees on Doctrine and Pastoral Research and Practices at the United States Conference of Catholic Bishops (USCCB).

Underlying all of his writings is the conviction that living religious belief comes out of the experience of grace, a living relationship with God that always includes an invitation to enter more deeply into the fullness of being found in friendship with God. God here is not merely a philosophical concept to be analyzed or a remote First Cause on whom the world depends, but the living, indwelling personal reality "in whom we live and move and have our being" (Acts 17:28). For Fr. Buckley, this God was disclosed most aptly by the mystics, and especially by St. John of the Cross.

We can come to experience God's presence when awestruck by the majesty of the natural world or inspired by the intellectual wonder that is the beginning of philosophy or stirred by moments of solitary contemplative prayer, but we are most likely to experience the presence of God in interpersonal encounters. On this point, Fr. Buckley's students have most profoundly felt the impact of his theology, because he has been for them not only a professor and advisor but also a mentor and friend. He has a deep love for the church and her sacramental life because it is here that we cultivate the kind of companionships that sustain and cultivate a living faith. We find grace most powerfully in the "union of hearts and minds" made possible by the communication of friends, the common life of religious communities, and the intimacy of marriage and family.

The present work is an expression of Fr. Buckley's abiding concern with the personal and interpersonal locus of authentic Christian faith. He asks his readers to pay attention to the ways in which Jesus invites his friends to come closer to God not by teaching them doctrines but by asking them to respond to certain apt, deliberately placed questions. Fr. Buckley's essential insight here resonates with that of Rabbi Abraham Joshua Heschel, who observed, "We are closer to God when we are asking questions than when we think we have the answers." *What Do You Seek?* provides a series of meditations on the questions posed by Jesus to his interlocutors in the Gospel of John. The chapters of this book are meant to challenge readers to take these questions personally and to consider themselves as called upon to formulate a concrete and honest response to Jesus's probing. We are at the same time asked to consider Jesus's questions as attempting to bring us to an awareness of our own deepest desires and therein to discover the presence of the Spirit in our lives and in the world. In a sense, then, we can see this work as the culmination of a lifetime of entering ever more deeply into the mystery of God through a probing of the deepest questions God poses to us.

Paul G. Crowley, SJ, and Stephen J. Pope

ACKNOWLEDGMENTS

These pages are obviously indebted to the reflections of scholars from the past and the present, as well as to the history of spirituality out of which they come. To all these, the author expresses his unfailing admiration and gratitude.

This slight volume, then, goes to press carrying a massive debt to the competence and generous kindness of others. Among these, several benefactors should especially be named to whom my gratitude is boundless: Sister Roberta Carson, SNJM, of the US-Ontario Province; Professor Stephen J. Pope of Boston College; Professor Paul Crowley, SJ, of Santa Clara University; the Jesuit Community of Sacred Heart Jesuit Center, Los Gatos, California; Tom Raabe, editor; and Angie Hollar of the Jesuit School of Theology at Santa Clara University.

To them, as well as to a vast number of friends and colleagues, I offer my sincere thanks and admiration.

INTRODUCTION

"If I tell you, you will not believe; and if I ask
you, you will not answer." (Luke 22:67–68)

Reclaiming the Vitality of Language

It seems many years ago now, that September conversation with an Oklahoma farmer. A careful, considered man, I thought. Years of hard work were written deep into the rough contours of his face and had worked their way into the dusty, stained creases in his overalls. Recent years had brought him within an ace of losing his farm to drought. Steady, implacable erosion was drying up the land. Each spring, he and his brothers would disk the earth and plant their crop. Each year, less would be forthcoming. Underneath the superficial topsoil, a hard compact of clay and rock was congealing, turning back the moisture struggling to push up from beneath the soil. The rain would hit this hard layer of clay, only to run off in rivulets. The field was becoming dust.

The brothers figured to abandon the tractor and its disks, build a plow with an outside blade that would cut deep into the earth, harness a powerful team of mules, and plow the field. This massive, metal plow could reach beneath the clay, slicing the impacted soil and rocks, breaking up heavy clods into smaller pieces. This would ease the moisture beneath, allowing the rainwater and roots to sink into the soil. When they did this, their yield was prolific, the best in memory.

The September sun was beating down hard upon us as the man told his story. I found myself drawn into it, recognizing how much of his narrative was also metaphor, a trope carrying much of a distant secret for one like myself, working reflectively within the mystery of God. Theologians, preachers, priests, and teachers write and talk so much about the Holy One, paradoxically revered as infinitely beyond words. Eventually, the endless prose, the usual religious words, the expected but actually quite manageable challenges grow old, anhydrous in their repetitions, in the public and parochial talk, in the debates and discussions of those who have come to know this language and its routines well. The reiterated words congeal into this overlay of hard clay. The stark gospel or demanding experiences obtain little purchase. God, as also the prose around "God," fades into the tediously banal and sterile.

George Steiner found such predictable religious prose constituting a world "rotten with lifeless clichés, with meaningless jargon, with intentional or unconscious falsehood."[1] Irretrievably dying in this formulaic sterility is the unutterable awe before the One who "dwells in unapproachable light" (1 Tim. 6:16).[2] For the mystery that encloses human lives and culture obtains little meaning when language has rendered the Divine dull and clichéd.

Still, Christians must talk about God. There is an urgency about this. For we think, communicate, and form all our societies only in language. Language is a humanizing gift. It permeates all the attempts of human beings to develop culture and to achieve a common meaning. As such, it is inescapable. What erodes into

1. George Steiner, *Real Presences* (Chicago: University of Chicago Press, 1989), 110–11.

2. Unless otherwise indicated, all biblical quotations in this book come from the Revised Standard Version.

the negative, however, is that human beings are talked at continually. The sheer quantity and repetition harden or exhaust or even corrupt the imagination, making appreciation, insight, and depth impossible. Time after time the maxim is verified: "You adopt the language and then the language adopts you." Human beings are the product of what they say and hear. Language can enhance, but it can also dangerously desiccate and destroy. And in this debasement, religious intensity and its sensibilities die.

The issue, then, inevitably confronts religious sensibilities, whether theological or evangelical: Is there any way in which the language about God, about religious experience before God, language from the Gospels themselves, can maintain its inherent vitality, can continue to convey life and human urgency? Is there any plow that can turn over this soil to reveal its native promise and fecundity? Is there any way in which the richness of religious statement and poetry can open human beings to the unspeakably sublime and escape the death of a thousand theological paragraphs?

Asking Questions

The Scriptures themselves could take the lead in this troubled search. The statements of Jesus in the Gospels, for example, often constitute a sharp, dark anticipation to be realized. In the Lukan passion narrative, during the morning trial before the entire assembly, Jesus advances his identity (Luke 22:66–71). His claims carry the meaning of what will come to pass. But this Lukan scene differs remarkably from that of Mark. In Luke, the entire Sanhedrin judges Jesus. He is being tried by those who speak for Israel, and his speech introduces what is to become an algorithm for the witness to be repeated by Peter and Stephen and Paul in the Acts of the Apostles. But something in Luke is very odd—something in the response of Jesus that has no parallel in the other Synoptics or in Acts. Jesus is asked if he is the Messiah, the fulfillment of God's promise to David. And he responds with a troubling, even pessimistic, statement: "If I tell you, you will not believe; and if I ask you (*ean de eroteso*), you will not answer" (22:67–68).

That Jesus would speak and not be believed is common enough in the Gospels and in subsequent religious and historical experience. It is the history of the church in the world. But that he would question the leaders of Israel about himself during his own trial, and that he would count a refusal to answer or engage him as equivalent to hostile disbelief—this draws a somewhat foreboding picture of Jesus, one strange and unique to this version of the Gospel.

It is strange, but paradoxically in remarkable continuity with his life in Luke's Gospel, that the first occasion Jesus is found speaking is as a questioner. He is only a child of twelve at the time, and is in the temple, "sitting among the teachers, listening to them and asking them questions (*eperotonta*)" (2:46). These teachers would answer the child; the Sanhedrin, many years later, would not answer the man. But both groups had to contend with the unsettling questions that came to them from Jesus. Both encountered this kind of priority, the inaugural priority of questioning over other forms of discourse in the Lukan Jesus's interchange with the world. In this string of interchanges, the question comes temporally first.

Much has been written about Jesus in contemporary Christian theology as one who proclaims the kingdom. Indeed, when trying to establish the nature of the self-consciousness of Jesus—what the earthly Jesus thought himself to be—Karl Rahner and Edward Schillebeeckx adopt the phrase "the eschatological prophet."

Another tradition, one that goes back to the formulation of the passion narratives, speaks of Jesus as the suffering servant of Isaiah: the one who suffers and dies for the salvation of human beings and for the redemption of Israel. Still another theme in contemporary Christology concentrates on Jesus as the risen Lord, the one who rises from the dead and gives the Spirit to those who believe in him: the one who baptizes with the Spirit.

Eschatological prophet, suffering servant, Spirit-giving Lord—one of these images does not contradict the other two, for they are more than complementary. One of these titles can actually lead into the others. Theologically they are organically related: Jesus became Lord and the source of the Spirit by moving in obedience and love through his sufferings, and these sufferings and death were those of the faithful prophet. Each title tells how Christian understanding develops toward its completion.

But there is another vision, another aspect of Jesus—one much less attended to, very much unexplored in contemporary theology and spirituality. This is the Jesus who at various critical moments is directly proclaiming nothing, explicitly teaching nothing. Rather, he frames a question within which a personal disclosure can occur, a question within which an interchange will occur or not occur, a question that those who encounter him must live with in the hiddenness of their own lives. Through these questions, Jesus directs those who encounter him back upon themselves, back into their own world. What do they find within themselves that responds to the probing interrogation that Jesus is leveling?[3] Such questions do not inform—they do not indoctrinate or urge. Such questions reach into a person and disclose what is already there, perhaps a fact about the person but uninterpreted. They turn the partners in this dialogue in upon themselves.

3. Some years ago I was regularly giving retreats, especially to religious. I formulated a program that centered each conference around a single question of Jesus in the Gospel of John. Over a period of years, the number of these lectures grew, and I was planning on editing and publishing them. When preparing this book for publication, I discovered that the talented poet and essayist John S. Dear had already crafted and published a series of meditation talks under the title *The Questions of Jesus*. John's reflections were specifically from the peace and justice perspective. When I wrote to John, he responded that the books were quite different and that I should not be concerned about his book and to publish as I had planned.

Questions That Probe for Meaning

To ask a question in this way is not to inform, not to furnish new areas of knowledge. It is rather to probe what is already there inside a human being, even if unrecognized. The Sermon on the Mount or the farewell discourse of the Last Supper may impart knowledge or commands. The questions of Jesus probe or encourage a knowledge or an experience that is in some way already there. They probe for meaning in the silent, interior world of those who hear them.

The Platonic tradition as found in the *Seventh Epistle* teaches that any serious question presupposes some coordination among fact and language and meaning. So the questioning of Jesus can search out the meaning of any religious experience, as well as the convictions and character of those who admit it. The question can probe what is central and pervasive in life. It can touch all the aspects that are implicated and included by this life. In this way, the question can open upon the Spirit of God that is present and directing human life in its interiority. The question can touch the depth of the person questioned, and as such it gathers to itself much of the experience that is contained within the life of the person questioned. For the answer—like the question—may not be outside of the person; it may be from within. And here precisely is its mystery. For, as Norman Maclean wrote on the tragedy of his brother's death, "How can a question be answered that asks a lifetime of questions?"[4] You do not answer such a question: your whole life is a quest for its response.

Think what is so simple, what is so ordinary, as to ask a question. What are human beings doing when they break into the current of another's life with a serious question, one that demands reflection? Further, what happens when one actually admits into

---

4. Timothy Foote, "A New Film about Fly Fishing—and Much, Much More," *Smithsonian* 23, no. 6 (September 1992): 122.

his or her own life such a disruptive moment, a searching question that may in its drive for a new awareness disconcert the easy pattern of reflection that had preceded it? Such a moment obviously entails the prior experiences of recognized ignorance, of a pause in assertions.

Its presence need not extend to encompass what would be simply new knowledge. Very often one draws from an experience or a fact already possessed, opaquely possessed, a new reception and understanding, but one so general or vague as to be inadequate. A question as such may not provide new instruction, new facts, or new data, however much it might incite a desire for these. The question may actually turn human beings reflexively back upon themselves—upon the experiences and commitments and beliefs that are taken to be there already but that cry out for understanding and meaning, upon a store of habits, convictions, data, decisions, and challenges. The question takes up what has been a challenge, what has been a sacred charge from the most ancient wisdom: "know yourself." For the question asks what is there already, even if unnoticed and unexplained.

For this "already" is what a person is—these habits from the past, these memories, these capacities, these longings and loves, these decisions, these convictions, this freedom—this self. This is the subjective world open to every question, the world in which persons live as subjects and possess themselves, the world into which the person ceaselessly receives and redefines new experiences and data. Questions draw a person back to herself, back to himself. Each serious question is some aspect of the more general question: Who are you? Each serious question gives a human being a chance for personal appropriation and disclosure as new information or proclamation does not.

Honest conviction of ignorance, as well as conviction of knowledge, lies at the origin of the honest question. If a human being allows into his or her consciousness the admission of ignorance, that is, if a human being takes a serious question seriously, then the person has little certitude of its further circumscriptions, what the consequent inquiry will gather into itself or where it will go. All that one must possess is the determination to face it out—to tell the truth with some confidence that even if there is uncertainty and fear here, it will eventually give way to a new freedom, the freedom to acknowledge the truth.

This supremacy of truth and conscience is the religious moment in every question. It initiates any honest inquiry and demands profound reverence.

Truth, then, is the supereminent mystery contained in or demanded by the questions of Jesus. They disclose to the reverent and attentive the mystery of their own lives as they disclose who Jesus is. For it is in the question that one encounters the Absolute, both in the direction in which it takes us and in the uncompromising demands it makes upon us, to unconditionally acknowledge the truth no matter what the cost. For when one unconditionally follows or surrenders to the truth simply because it is the truth, one encounters an irrefragable claim made upon oneself. Nothing can take its place. Nothing can break its imperial and legitimate claim over human conscience. It is an experience of the Absolute. Truth given this utter adherence is an attribute of God. And it is classically true in Catholic theology that human beings come to know God in his attributes. This summons to truth issues from the very heart of the question. To be brought to acknowledge the primordial imperative and supremacy of truth is to come to recognize the presence and claim of God.

Question and Parable

In 1990 Alfred A. Knopf published the memoirs of the celebrated playwright and the first elected president of the Czech Republic, Václav Havel, entitled *Disturbing the Peace*. These memoirs were derived from months of conversation with Karel Hvizdala.

Hvizdala was living in West Germany and Havel in Prague in 1985. Hvizdala sent Havel a set of fifty questions, and Havel shut himself up in a borrowed flat in order to compose his answers. The translator, Paul Wilson, says that Havel liked the project because these questions "gave him a chance to reflect upon his life as he approached fifty."[5] He saw so much of the promise of his life evoked by these questions: "I am a writer, and I've always understood my mission to be to speak the truth about the world I live in."[6] The questions allowed him to focus on his world and its values with what Christians have learned to call purity of heart.

The same motivation draws Christians to attend to the questions of Jesus. How do we answer this man who stands before us throughout the Gospels in his unique spirit? Perhaps these questions of Jesus are most like his parables; perhaps they serve a similar purpose—like a deep plow plunging into hard soil, they split life open.

For what is a parable of Jesus? C. H. Dodd maintains that each parable is: "(a) A metaphor or a simile, (b) drawn from nature or common life, (c) arresting the hearers by its vividness or strangeness, (d) leaving the mind in sufficient doubt about its precise application, (e) to tease it into active thought."[7]

The questions of Jesus bear much of the same character and urgency. Like a parable, a question from Jesus may also initiate (a) an inquiry (a probe or a problem posed by Jesus), (b) drawn from the course of the life emerging around him, (c) arresting the hearers by its challenge or its redirection of attention back to their awareness of what is within, (d) leaving the mind in sufficient doubt about the precise or adequate answer, (e) even disturbing the mind into active thought and recognition—or, more profoundly, into prayer and the consciousness of the presence and call of God.

5. Václav Havel, *Disturbing the Peace: A Conversation with Karel Hvizdala,* trans. Paul Wilson (New York: Knopf, 1990), vii–ix.

6. Havel, *Disturbing the Peace,* 8.

7. C. H. Dodd, *Parables* (New York: Charles Scribner's Sons, 1961).

The parable leads one to a critical reappraisal: How does this have meaning and how is it realized in my life? The question opens one to a double challenge: How do I find and define myself in answer to this question? And this means, more immediately: How do I answer this man?

Perhaps, in this sense, the dual character of the questions makes them more interpersonal—more immediately prayerful. They are both challenge and promise. They are challenge because they force persons back upon the hiddenness within themselves. They demand, even at great personal cost, an honest response. One sees repeatedly in the Gospels that these questions summon human beings to account for themselves to themselves; to account for what has meaning and value in their lives.

But they are also a haunting promise, because the One who leads us on this journey into the unknown is "always greater"; he is the mystery that calls to us more deeply and loves us more wisely. This conviction may often be hidden from our eyes. But it is the horizon and the promise of those lives that we do not yet see. It is the very reason for the questioning. We are drawn by the question.

One comes to the questions of Jesus much as T. S. Eliot approached Little Gidding, the monastic chapel of Nicholas Ferrar and his seventeenth-century Anglican religious community, destroyed by Cromwell's troops in 1646. Approaching this stripped and utterly bare chapel, Eliot writes:

> You are not here to verify,
> Instruct yourself, or inform curiosity
> Or carry report. You are here to kneel
> Where prayer has been valid.[8]

---

8. T. S. Eliot, "Little Gidding," in *The Complete Poems and Plays, 1909–1950* (San Diego: Harcourt Brace Jovanovich, 1971), 138.

The questions of Jesus are where prayer has always been valid. The initiative is already and always his. The empowered response under grace is ours. In his questions Jesus holds us within his gaze.

The Purpose of This Book

The purpose of this book is to attend to some of these questions of Jesus.

Each of the Gospels presents this aspect of Jesus—his questioning, searching character. The reflections in this book will engage only one Gospel, the Gospel of John, and only a few of the questions it places before us. Thirty-five times in the Gospel of John, Jesus levels critical questions at the life of human beings, as to the meaning of what we say, of what we do, and of what we are. Indeed, as Jesus emerges in this Gospel, he leads human beings back to themselves, back to their own religious depths and unfaced attitudes, back into their own worlds and individual histories and the crucial action of God within themselves. In any attempt to respond, the questions gradually bring to the surface what meaning life has for those who would hear them, what is the spirit in which they live and which gives their lives meaning. In other words, the questions of Jesus lead the attentive to recognize what God is doing in their lives; that is, the character, the world, and the vocation of their lives—as well as the life of the Spirit within them bringing them to the mystery of their own union with God.

In this Johannine narrative, the very first question of Jesus discloses the fundamental desires, the longings that energize the commitments evoked by the radical inquiries and experience of Jesus. Each of these questions in its fullness bespeaks the other questions in the life, death, public ministry, and resurrection of Jesus. Yet no attempt is made here to reduce all these questions to a single narrative, to a concatenated sequence in which the members build subsequently upon other members. It is better to see these questions as constituting in the Gospel, not a single developing narrative, but more a field of force.[9] This is to suggest that the questions of Jesus should be addressed neither as a simple developmental hypothesis nor as a logistic scheme. Each of the questions is both single and universal; each bespeaks the whole, the entire life of those who hear it as well as the entire life of the One who poses it. For these reasons it seemed advantageous to understand these questions of Jesus not as a single developmental scheme but, as indicated above, as a field of force.

Drawn to the Spirit

As human beings come to recognize and assimilate these questions, they enter into the field of force constituted by these questions. They do not so much take in more knowledge from the outside as they are drawn into attention to the Spirit that is already within their lives but unrecognized. The questions of Jesus, if heard, draw them into the reverence evoked by the Spirit of God at work in their world. Jesus in this way becomes the plow that turns over their lives, disclosing a presence that is divine.

The Christian, standing before the questioning Jesus, knows that this self-knowledge is not simply the Socratic "know thyself." It is this and much more. Far more important is the interior vocation of Jesus to appropriate the love and the direction of the Spirit of Jesus—the indwelling Spirit that configures a person or a community to Christ and so allows Jesus to direct these lives to God. This is to live within the Spirit—to attempt to respond as a disciple of Jesus Christ. In the presence of the Spirit Jesus becomes method.

9. "Field theories use mathematical quantities such as vectors or tensors to describe how the conditions at any point in space will affect matter of another field. For example, in a gravitational or a magnetic field there are articles that could act upon a particle at any point." Walter Isaacson, *Einstein* (New York: Simon and Schuster, 2008), 92.

Perhaps, then, all human beings can allow the questions of Jesus to seep like water on dry earth into their consciousness. So they challenge their lives, as they can find themselves searched by the One who has called out to them.

This seems to have been the formative experience of Dag Hammarskjöld: "I don't know Who—or what—put the question. I don't know when it was put. I don't even remember answering. But at some moment, I did answer Yes to Someone—or Something— and from that hour I was certain that existence is meaningful and therefore my life in self surrender had a goal. From that moment I have known what it means 'not to look back' and 'to take no thought for the morrow.'"[10]

10. Dag Hammarskjöld, *Markings*, trans. Leif Sjöberg and W. H. Auden (New York: Knopf, 1964), 205.

⚜(1)⚜

"WHAT DO YOU SEEK?"

> *The next day again John was standing with*
> *two of his disciples; and he looked at Jesus as*
> *he walked, and said, "Behold, the Lamb of*
> *God!" The two disciples heard him say this,*
> *and they followed Jesus. Jesus turned, and*
> *saw them following, and said to them, "What*
> *do you seek?"* (John 1:35–38)

The First Question

The first words of Jesus in this Gospel—"What do you seek?"—
deliver a question and frame a world. They do not simply allow
the recognition of a new fact; they inquire into what has been
suggested but only begun to be recognized—the comprehensive
hope that was to become Christianity. This question of Jesus is
put very deliberately, if indistinctly. It will raise those who hear it
to a world and to a communion that only he can form with them.

In the Gospel, Jesus turns and gazes at John's followers, and his
gaze transforms this encounter into an epiphany. His attention is
upon them. This gaze of Jesus on these first disciples initiates their
consciousness into something profoundly yet unthematically within

them. Only this transformation will make sense of the question they would later put to Jesus: "To whom should we go?" This touches their vague emptiness, their longings, and the search that has been in some way with them over time. All this falls under his gaze.

This gaze of Jesus—not speculation or religious argument—constitutes the first and fundamental invitation to discipleship. The later-developing familiarity with Jesus in the Gospel will call this gaze into play more intensely. The gaze will bespeak the vision of Jesus at the dawning in human life of the incarnate Word with which the prologue to the Gospel opens: "And the Word became flesh and dwelt among us, full of grace and truth; we have [gazed at (*etheasametha*)] his glory, glory as of the only Son from the Father" (1:14). Now, however, in this first narrative of Jesus in the Gospel of John, it is not the disciples who first gaze at Jesus, but Jesus who first gazes on them, upon these two men that the Gospel will describe as "following him."

It is important to grasp this action, of Jesus's holding these men in his vision. The religious depth of the question he will place before them can only be ascertained within this gaze. The urgency of this question will be disclosed and accepted only in the gaze that will grow into love, friendship, and community. Only when the gaze of Jesus is recognized as the context for everything that follows are fidelity and authentic discipleship possible.

The religious significance of this early moment must not be minimized. When Ignatius of Loyola gave introductory directions for the beginnings of prayer, he did not urge those engaged in his *Spiritual Exercises,* called exercitants, to begin by calling to mind that God is present—though such advice is commonplace in standard meditation manuals. They were to initiate the period of formal prayer in this way: "I will raise my mind to consider: How it is that God our Lord"—Ignatius's phrase for Christ—"is gazing at me (*como me mira*)."[1] For Ignatius, the human contemplation

---

1. Ignatius of Loyola, *The Spiritual Exercises of St. Ignatius: A Literal Trans-*

of God always takes place and is only made possible within a recognition of God's prior contemplation of human beings. The humanity of Christ has made this gaze of Jesus possible. In this gaze, Jesus holds these men who are following him within this question that can be so variously translated: *"ti zeteite?"*—"What are you seeking?" "What are you looking for?" "What do you want?" (cf. John 1:38).

The Gospel situates questions of purpose and meaning within fundamental interpersonal desire. The human longing for God is awakened by God's desire for the human person. What is to be understood later in this Gospel narrative about the action of God or the Spirit of God must be understood within this prior attention or reverence given human beings by Jesus through these questions. He is active first, before any human choice or action. He chooses people; they do not first choose him (15:16). For in prayer God is more profoundly subject than object, more agent than passive recipient. In this, Jesus most profoundly embodies the presence and activity of God. God's gaze upon human beings constitutes the possibility for divine revelation, for a human response, and for intersubjective communion with him. Jesus will recognize and elicit the absolutely fundamental human desire for God; he will locate his gospel, his "good news," here in this primary awareness. Thus his initial question must disclose the longing for God, however indistinctly present in the humanity of every human being.

This first and foundational question in the Gospel of John is one that Jesus will repeat urgently, and in some transmuted way, at the two pivotal junctures of the Gospel. This repetition and location underlines its preeminence and its thematic seriousness for anyone contemplating the Gospel narrative.

The Gospel will also initiate the passion with this recognition by Jesus of what the future holds for him: "Jesus, knowing all that

lation and a Contemporary Reading, trans. Elder Mullan, SJ (St. Louis: Institute of Jesuit Sources, 1978), 50.

was to befall him, came forward and said to them, 'Whom do you seek?'" (18:4). This question achieves more focus; and this in turn initiates the sequences that will lead to and through the passion. Jesus emerges from the garden and twice puts the same question to the soldiers who are to take him to his death. Finally, at the very beginning of the resurrection appearances, as Mary stands weeping outside the empty tomb, Jesus's first words are: "Woman, why are you weeping? Whom do you seek?" (20:15). The beginning of his public life, the entrance into his passion, the first of his resurrection appearances—each of these crucial thematic events opens with this question about search and desire. All probe for longing and yearning. That is where it all begins.

The Priority of the Question

Why does John place this as the very first question in the Gospel? Because, as Rudolf Bultmann has wisely written: "It is clearly the first question that must be addressed to anyone who comes to Jesus, the first thing that must be clear."[2] The Gospel does not make it precisely a moment of information for Jesus. In a very few verses of this narrative, he will indicate that he can read hearts and size up the character of Simon and the straightforward innocence of Nathaniel (1:42–47). No, the question is not for him; it is for them. It is for these people who would come to follow him—if they would follow him.

This question throws them back upon themselves, and calls them to attend to their own religious experience and to the narrative in which their experiences are enclosed. They are carried by the question to see what is the mystery that draws them, what actually has value for them, what has made them decide on this direction

2. Rudolf Bultmann, *The Gospel of John: A Commentary*, trans. G. R. Beasley-Murray, R. W. N. Hoare, and J. K. Riches (Philadelphia: Westminster, 1971), 100.

rather than on another. The question then guides them to come to a profound awareness of themselves, and to understand themselves in their own desires; to know who they are and what they are to become. For their meaning only emerges as they come into a consciousness of what they most deeply desire. Only their desires can ascend into the freedom and the courage to follow him. For only here—beneath and deeper than immediate appetite and the multiple distortions of self-congratulatory motivation—are there grace and a new freedom that Paul would come to celebrate as "God's love has been poured into our hearts through the Holy Spirit which has been given to us" (Rom. 5:5). It is this desire, this love, that he has initially awakened in those who would follow him. It will gather strength in the years to come in companionship and community.

Love, classically, can exist in one of two ways, but "love" as an abstraction never exists; love is always concrete, whether in action or in passion. Concretely love exists either when you possess the one you love, and then love exists as joy; or when you do not possess the one you love, and then love exists as desire—as yearning—as longing—and as search. Desire and joy, in their strength, reveal to human beings what really matters deeply in their lives. In this way they find out who they are. What human beings really love is what gives their years and their lives purpose, direction, and contour.[3] This is why Jesus must probe for desire as the Gospel opens—What is it you love? Who are you?

This question of Jesus to his disciples excavates beneath actions and external performance, beneath what people ascribe to one another, beneath what is counted as success or failure. It probes for an underlying and comprehensive longing—"what is drawing me; what do I want?" The question of Jesus attempts to bring to the surface the desires that are actually governing human life. It reaches into hope for the joy that gives everything human beings touch expectation and meaning.

3. Thomas Aquinas, *Summa Theologiae* II, q. 28, a. 4.

This love and this desire constitute, in Heidegger's term, the *Urfrage*, the basic human question. It underlies every dynamism that informs and drives an entire life. This question can emerge at any place in human lives. As in this passage, it can begin with an almost casual walk. It can emerge from any action that suddenly catches human beings up in shame or in wonder, in expectation or fear or love, or in the most pedestrian moments of a usual day. The journey inward to search out what we are looking for is a very long one. Dag Hammarskjöld was wise to write: "The longest journey is the journey inward."[4] Sometimes, it is almost impossible to say where human beings are traveling or why they are questioning. "Self-appropriation" is ruthlessly demanding when it touches on real motives, and as the process of questioning foreshadows within us a massive world of values and culture that has become more and more murky.[5]

Human beings can build up answers to justify action or to alibi the mixture of motives actually present—operative motives half seen and so often shamefully self-serving or defensive or hostile or ambitious or false. But human beings may also be equally or even pervasively unwilling to acknowledge the good and grace already worked in their hearts, in their desires and joys. It is a real threat to human life that human beings may denigrate or ignore the extensive field of grace in which they live and move and have their being (Acts 17:28). Religious skepticism tends to dismiss all of this cynically as "too good to be true." But in this way, one defrauds the presence and the gift of God by measuring out the divine by "coffee spoons"[6] and by insistent interpretations that bespeak pettiness

4. Dag Hammarskjöld, *Markings*, trans. Leif Sjöberg and W. H. Auden (New York: Knopf, 1964), 58.

5. For more on self-appropriation, see Bernard Lonergan, *Insight: A Study in Human Understanding* (New York: Harper and Row, 1978).

6. T. S. Eliot, "The Love Song of J. Alfred Prufrock," in *The Complete Poems and Plays, 1909–1950* (San Diego: Harcourt Brace Jovanovich, 1971), 5:

For I have known them all already, known them all: —
Have known the evenings, mornings, afternoons,

and limitations. And yet, over and over again, human beings can be brought to see that underneath everything there is a longing for God that is actually sacred—however distorted by disordered affectivity this longing has become. This first question of Jesus in the Gospel of John is supremely important, however inadequate the human response. Even this inadequacy should not deter the Christian, for "God is greater than our hearts, and he knows everything" (1 John 3:20).

Christian wisdom has insisted upon this fundamental question of desire in a thousand ways since the first centuries. In the great *Conferences of the Abbot Moses*, John Cassian has Moses put this as the first and fundamental interrogation to those who came to him in the desert for instruction: "You have left your kinsfolk and your fatherland and the delights of this world, and passed through so many countries, in order that you might come to us, plain and simple folk as we are, living in this wretched state in the desert. Therefore, answer and tell me: what is the goal and the end which incites you to endure all of these things so cheerfully?"[7] Moses is probing for the same architectonic that Jesus is probing for: his question underlies passion and appetite, rational desire, search and quest, and the cost of discipleship—so that Moses will not accept the general answer "the kingdom of God." He will insist upon something more immediate, more concrete: "If we have not in similar fashion grasped this we shall be wearied fruitlessly by our toil, because if the road is uncharted, then those who undertake the hardships of the journey will have nothing to show for it."[8]

This sober wisdom has been treasured and practiced within

I have measured out my life with coffee spoons;
I know the voices dying with a dying fall
Beneath the music from a farther room.
    So how should I presume?

7. *John Cassian: The Conferences*, trans. Boniface Ramsey, OP (New York: Paulist, 1997), conference I, section 2, paragraph 3, p. 42.

8. *John Cassian: The Conferences*, conference I, section 4, paragraph 1, p. 43.

the spirituality of the church for many centuries. When a man applied for admission into a monastery, Benedict directed the master of novices to examine the candidate exactingly for motive. "The concern should be whether he truly seeks God."[9] These masters of radical Christian living were to explore desire carefully and critically. For they believed that the deepest human longing (albeit often misinterpreted and misguided) is for God, that human beings are made for God, and that this insatiable hunger still remains no matter how distorted affectivity, desires, and motivations become. This desire for God is the root of everything religious.

Growth in the Spirit takes wing when it appropriates this radical longing for God—when it sees what specifies human beings. Perceptively, the great French theologian Louis Lallement wrote that "There is a void in our heart which all creatures united would be unable to fill. God alone can fill it; for He is our beginning and our end."[10] In the darkness of confused and unfulfilled desires, the spirit and the silence of God align human motivations with these singular longings of the heart for God. Here human beings move toward a more profound and pervasive purity of heart; they come into a peace, a more specifying integrity, a deeper and a cleaner joy. This initial question of Jesus in the Gospel probes for this focus of desire—perhaps painfully; however, it can demand much and include much. It works upon human consciousness because human beings will discover under all disorder and compromise and discouragement that a greater love is to be realized.

Only this greater love can put order into the lesser loves—the way that a bar magnet can draw iron filings into a pattern. This question of Jesus calls those who hear it into a radical integrity and direction, culminating in a purity of heart and freedom. It is a call

9. Latin text: "sit si revera Deum quaerit." Benedict of Nursia, *Rule of Benedict*, ed. and trans. Bruce L. Venarde (Cambridge, MA: Harvard University Press, 2011), 187.

10. Louis Lallement, *The Spiritual Doctrine*, trans. Frederick William Faber, DD (London: Levey, Robson and Franklyn, 1855), 37.

to see that it is Christ whom human beings want—God's incarnate self-communication to human lives—and in comparison to this, everything else is negotiable.

Human beings and divergent cultures can reformulate his question as they will—so long as it includes radical desire, a love that is total and encompassing, self-transcendence, and comprehensive search: "What do you want out of life?" "What sustains in your life now a sense of meaning and habitual joy?" "When death comes, what will you want your life to have meant?" Human beings answer such questions always in parts. They stammer out their responses in fragments over time. As these fragments become more authentic, they rise in human consciousness. They can become so vast that one can only stammer a few sentences and then wait for more to emerge from inside oneself.

Above all, it is crucial to recognize both in this Gospel and in the total life of the Christian, that it is Christ who asks this question, the One the book of Revelation describes as "him who loves us and has freed us from our sins by his blood and made us a kingdom, priests to his God and Father" (Rev. 1:5–6). In his gaze, the first event of discipleship, human beings can gain the quiet courage to hear and respond to the searching quality of the foundational question: "What are you looking for? What do you seek?" At the beginning of his great digression on contemplation in the third book of the *Living Flame of Love*, John of the Cross expresses the convictions that ground everything he will subsequently say: "First it must be known that, if the soul is seeking God, its Beloved is seeking it much more."[11]

---

11. John of the Cross, *Living Flame of Love*, trans. E. Allison Peers (London: Burns and Oates, 1977), 175.

⤙ 2 ⤚

"DO YOU KNOW WHAT I HAVE DONE TO YOU?"

When [Jesus] had washed their feet, and
taken his garments, and resumed his place,
he said to them, "Do you know what I have
done to you?" (John 13:12)

A Question of Awareness

This is not a statement. It is a question. It doesn't directly assert anything, doesn't deliver anything new to assimilate, doesn't even insinuate new data from the outside. Rather, it suggests much that in prospect should have shaken the disciples. Jesus asks them what they are already conscious of—what they have experienced and inchoately understood, perhaps talked about and lived with—what they find in some way or other inside themselves and their world after this very strange moment in which Jesus washed their feet. What is in question is their depth and awareness—how much they have become aware of the mystery working influentially within their lives, over the many weeks that have preceded the present moment.

This question of awareness is central to the reverence that must be native to authentic Christianity. Repeatedly, in some alternate form, it has been posed urgently or even reproachfully by human

beings. But now—perhaps for the first time—the question of attention and reverence is placed before human beings by Jesus himself.
He insists upon the answer that will disclose to them their lived
relationship with God himself, upon the character of a dawning
awareness of the divine in this human being that is primordial for
all that is contained in Christianity. Eternal life is to be understood,
not so much as endless perduration, but as a new kind of experiential consciousness: "This is eternal life, that they know thee the
only true God, and Jesus Christ whom thou hast sent" (John 17:3).
The question comes to this: What are you aware of in your life? Are
you conscious of the mysterious actions of God within you? This
searching inquiry has a long history in Christianity.

This is the mystery evoked from Ignatius of Loyola in the third
point of *The Contemplation to Attain Love* in the *Spiritual Exercises.* As the days of the spiritual exercises move to their completion, they indicate for one engaged in those exercises, called an
exercitant, ultimate days that are to deepen into "inward knowledge" (*conocimiento interno*) the principal themes of the previous
weeks of contemplative prayer. They do so in a comprehensive
contemplation that focuses upon the reality of God and upon the
totality of his presence and action within the world. They name
the divine action so that the exercitant may come in everything to
"love and serve the Divine Majesty." The contemplation gathers to
its strength and moves through four progressive points.

As the first focus for the specific prayer and contemplation
of the exercitant, God is reverenced and adored as the infinite
source of all beings, of all creation and of salvation, and indeed, of
every good thing. With a generosity whose extension can only be
divine, God gives to human lives whatever they possess, even gives
them himself. To understand creation, it is crucially necessary for
the exercitant in the *Exercises* to recognize that whatever human
beings come to possess is a wonderment given them by God. All
things are gifts, to be contemplated foundationally in their ontological density, to be appropriated as the gifts of God. "Gift" is the
universal and fundamental Christian transcendental. This allows

one to move in appreciation from God giving all things, to God as actively present in all things.

All things are not only gifts, they are also holy. The gifts of creation are fundamentally sacred and bear this imprint of God. The gratuity and the holiness of things recapitulate the first and second weeks of the *Exercises*, and both are founded upon a sense of the imperishable sacredness and vitality of all that is given and by the gratuitous presence of the Holy Spirit within them.

In the history of religions, much metaphysical doctrine and teaching has insisted upon all things as gifts of God. In addition, religious and even mystical experience has brought to a human awareness God's dwelling in all things, so that in this way all things are recognized as sacred. Either of these first two points of the *Contemplatio* can be found in widely divergent religious traditions and even in contradictory philosophies. But the third stage of the *Contemplatio*, that "God works in and through all things"; that he "struggles" in a very real if analogous sense, as the galaxies move; that the rush of all life is symptomatic of his sacred toil; that all things are caught up in the providential and redemptive work of God—this is not so universally appreciated. But it is emphatic in the *Exercises*. God "labors" in all things in order to effect salvation; the unity of all creation is with God. His labors are in this way salvific. The attempt to read the divine working, to interpret and understand all things as caught up in this divine labor and direction, bears upon any contemplative apostolic life. It is the radical discernment of the salvific presence and directions of God, permeating all that is. To read reality in this way is one of the forms of the Christian discernment of spirits, and to offer oneself as an instrument of this divine labor lies at the heart of the Ignatian life. These three points of the *Contemplatio* speak to the dynamic presence of God in all things. All three respond to the uniqueness of the question of Jesus: "Do you know what I have done to you?"[1]

---

1. See Michael J. Buckley, SJ, "The Contemplation to Attain Love," *The Way* Supplement 24 (Spring 1975): 92–104.

This questioning fosters a radical attention to fundamental religious experience and guidance—into the providential care of God. It reaches beyond the moment in the Upper Room and past the quotidian lives of the disciples. It probes religious sensibility and awareness, giving body to what otherwise might be reduced to an abstract and dogmatic assertion: "Do you know what has happened to you?" Even more personally, "Do you know what I have done to you?" The call is to a reverent religious awareness and love. Stop what you are doing—pause, turn to consider your life, and attend to some of the thousand things that have entered into your life from the formative time you were a child, things you have forgotten or now take for granted. Allow your reflection to come into the present. Notice how everything that has found its place in this review has antecedently shaped you. All is finally gift; all is finally sacred; all is finally providential. For this ceaseless care of God, the response is endless gratitude.

The alternative is to be religiously jaded—as when nine lepers never return, never recognize that their good is from another (Luke 17:17). This question perdures into the present. Jesus asks his disciples to attend to the grace that has come into their lives, that he has so often washed their feet and purified their histories. Christians can recognize Christ in these several histories: Christ in and through his Spirit has drawn them to God, baptized them in the Trinity, forgiven them, shaped their histories and their promise, called them to the life they are living, "eternal life," and to the joy that brings love to its completion and lasts forever. In this way, he calls them to a life of holiness, of union with God, sustains them in that life, and destines them to be with him forever.

Must not Christians come to recognize, in what is happening to them, what they hope for as "the time of their visitation"? For this visitation is a call to a blessed understanding of all human lives, to salvific awareness, to a pervasive care that Hopkins celebrates in "The Lantern out of Doors." For, in contrast with the indifference of human beings to each other:

> Christ minds; Christ's interest,
>> what to avow or amend
> There, éyes them, heart wánts,
>> care haúnts, foot fóllows kínd.
> Their ránsom, théir rescue,
>> and first, fást, last friend.[2]

In John's Gospel, this awareness was finally to be the experience of all who would come to him. Jesus had said that his sheep could and would follow him because they would recognize his voice (10:4). He had said that he would know them and that they would know him (10:14). This mysterious sensibility, with all its knowledge and awareness, would mean that they were no longer servants but friends. For the mark of the servant is that he does not know what the master is doing (15:15). It was this friendship, this recognition that would contrast with the terrible condemnation that John the Baptist would level at the religious elite, at the Pharisees: "among you stands one whom you do not know" (1:26). Every human being faces the question of Jesus: "Do you know what I have done to you?" Recognition, discernment, reverence is what is decisively at issue.

Prevenient Grace and the Mystery of Its Recognition

In 1921, Baron Friedrich von Hügel delivered a critically important lecture, "The Facts and Truths concerning God and the Soul Which Are of the Most Importance in the Life of Prayer." In this lecture, von Hügel insisted upon the primacy to be accorded the "prevenient grace of God" as the root fact and the fundamental truth of all that can be said about God's care for human beings: "God not only loves us more and better than we can ever love ourselves . . .

---

2. Gerard Manley Hopkins, "The Lantern out of Doors," in *Poems and Prose* (New York: Penguin, 1985), 28.

but God has loved us *before* we loved, or could love, Him." The prevenient grace of God is the absolutely antecedent and unmerited love that God has visited upon human beings, the grace prior to anything human beings have done. Prevenient grace marks the love of God for human beings in its highest gratuity. God has acted first.

Von Hügel made this awareness fundamental for a life of prayer: that God has acted on us—that "God [is] the true inspirer of our most original-seeming thoughts and wishes, when so ever these are good and fruitful—as He who secretly initiates what He openly crowns."[3]

The gratitude that responds to this prevenient grace is the created root of all Christian life and vocation. All the forms of Christian community and all the modalities of the Christian vocation are found here in forms that are widely variant as responses to this prior gift of Christ—the self-communication of God through the gift of his Spirit. Through this antecedent gift of his Spirit, Christ initiates all, every personal human initiative. These live in any Christian commitment. But perhaps Christian theology has not sufficiently stressed what makes the reception of this call of God even possible. What gives such a mysterious influence of God its intelligibility, its urgency, and its shape? It is the prior experience and awareness of having been touched—called, directed, loved, and cared for—by the Spirit of God. Only in this way can any Christian, or the church, ever come to an understanding of the shape of discipleship to which he or she is called. This fundamental experience of the Spirit makes the life of discipleship possible. The prior experience of having been effectively affected by God and drawn to God culminates in a love that is indistinguishable from the experience of being called to God, from the consciousness that God wants us for himself.

One can hear this summons to the life of intimate discipleship in so many different ways and on so many different levels of con-

---

3. Baron Friedrich von Hügel, *Essays and Addresses on the Philosophy of Religion: Second Series* (New York: Dutton, 1930), 225.

scious reception, moments of contemplative vision and love and necessarily longing and determination in which one is aware of an absolute call upon one's life without recognizing at the same time how infinitely personal and free it is. There are Christians who are anonymous, and so there are comprehensive, if hidden, movements toward God that shape the entire life of a human being. Such an experience can emerge as the articulation of a monastic vocation, or as marriage, or as service and solitude, or as one of the infinite varieties of ministerial services and responsibilities. In a Christian community this call is particularized as one answers this question of Jesus: "Do you know what I have done to you?"

This experience of the prior care of Christ for us is the fundamental experience that makes any life of Christian ministry possible. Otherwise this "call" becomes only a career. A person, or even a community, can hear the call to apostolic ministry only if he or she understands and assimilates how deeply, how much prior, Christ has been caring for and ministering to the person throughout his or her life.[4] His prior ministry to people makes possible their ministry to others, whatever form it takes. This is the fundamental teaching of both the Synoptics and John. It is the antecedent and crucial experience that lies at the base of all Christian ministry. Repeatedly it is asserted:

> "Let the greatest among you become as the youngest, and the leader as one who serves . . . [*Why?*] [because] I am among you as one who serves." (Luke 22:26–27)

> "As I have loved you [*Have you experienced this?*], that you also love one another." (John 13:34)

4. These convictions, with their supporting texts, are obviously much indebted to the scholarship of Louis Cameli as presented in his *Ministerial Consciousness: A Biblical-Spiritual Study* (Rome: Università Gregoriana Editrice, 1975). This splendid, solid work offers a rich exploration of the themes of the relationship between the ministry of Christ and the ministers in his church.

"If I . . . have washed your feet [*If you have experienced this*], you also ought to wash one another's feet. For I have given you an example, that you also should do as I have done to you." (John 13:14–15)

These interchanges demand that one ask, first of all, about the experience in love and the consciousness of a prior care, that of Jesus toward us. This is absolutely first. This prior, prevenient, ministerial love of Christ is the experiential basis of all Christian service and ministry. Only under its influence and as a response to it can one talk about a Christian care of others and about a charity that continues what one has learned from Christ.

What this Upper Room pericope is not asserting is that Christ is a religious or ethical model, one that does not actually touch my life, something outside of the deepest levels of my experience. It is not as if he were commanding, "Love and commit yourselves to the love of others because that constitutes Christian discipleship, it is the highest law." Taken by itself, as if it were enough—such service becomes almost the practice and the essence of Pelagianism. It is law and we are to measure up.

Jesus is saying something far more immediate and far more religious: he is calling upon the experience of what he has done to *you*, the experience that makes possible your understanding and the capacity for *your* life to care for others similarly. Each person's discipleship becomes possible only in this way. Christian ministry is not an adoption of certain practices within human lives; rather it is a continuation within our lives of what constitutes the life and the choices in the life of Jesus of Nazareth. Christian ministry is not so much a copying of the life of Jesus as it is a continuation of it.[5]

As Christians have experienced the Spirit imparted to them by the ministerial Christ, so they can continue his charity. But if

5. Cameli, *Ministerial Consciousness*, 28.

30

you have never attended to this experience of his care and ministry to you—that he has washed your feet, that he has been in your midst as one who serves you, that he has loved you first—if you have never appropriated this experience, then Christian discipleship is impossible. One can take up any number of practices and responsibilities because they are obviously good, but this is not Christian discipleship. Essential is the prior recognition that you are continuing in your life and in the lives of others what you recognize you have experienced of Christ.

This appropriation through the Spirit of what Christ has done and is doing in our lives issues in gratitude—a life of thanksgiving and of Eucharist: "And from the many gifts You have given us, we offer to You, God of Glory and Majesty, this holy and perfect sacrifice, the bread of life, the cup of eternal salvation."[6] This makes the Eucharist the soul of all following of Christ, of all discipleship and ministry. This is true, not just in the sense that these are realized in the Eucharist, but that the prevenient grace and gratitude embodied in the Eucharist are the root experience that makes our response possible. All this in some way lies behind Jesus's question to his disciples and to us: "Do you know what I have done to you?"

6. This line is contained in Eucharistic Prayer I.

⚜ 3 ⚜

"DO YOU BELIEVE IN THE SON OF MAN?"

Jesus heard that they had driven [the man who had been born blind] out, and when he found him, he said, "Do you believe in the Son of Man?" He answered, "And who is he, sir? Tell me, so that I may believe in him." Jesus said to him, "You have seen him, and the one speaking to you is he." He said, "Lord, I believe." And he worshiped him.
(John 9:35–38 NRSV)

Darkness within and Without

Perhaps for the first time in American history, an intermediate darkness attenuates and obscures much of the hope that once gave vitality and even enthusiasm to the Catholic Church in the United States. Depreciation has become a form of accepted realism, an extensive sphere of negative convictions about the church, its ministers, and its ecclesial constitution, supported, strengthened, and fed by an easy cynicism with no alleviation in sight. Over these past decades, Catholics have watched the media progressively discredit an uninspiring, superannuated celibate clergy with sordid tales of infidelity, pedophilia, overbearing and ignorant clumsiness, and venality. These have come to form an inescapable atmosphere in which those given to any form of ministerial or priestly dedication attempt to sustain their own commitment and to minister to an increasingly alienated and scandalized faithful. Over this last half-century, Catholics have become almost inured to an unspoken cultural contempt, to easy forms of public ridicule so common that they fail to contest them. The great negation pressing against the church today in the United States on the part of many is not so much disbelief as disgust, embarrassment, and dismissal.

Many things once taken for granted, celibacy and ecclesial obedience, for example, now yield to negations in theory and radical denials in practice. The number of "practicing Catholics" falls off. The median age of priests and sisters advances. Convents continue to close. Large novitiates have stood empty for decades. Depression has settled like dense fog upon once optimistic religious communities and projects. Ministers of the church wonder openly about its local governments and future. Leadership often seems maladroit, political, or woefully naïve and irremediably out of touch.

So much of what the church once easily possessed—public credibility, the unquestioned reputation of its priests and religious, an immediate admiration and understanding of its ethical and social teachings, a respected position in society for its moral influence, a security for itself and its leadership, and even a certain amount of acclaim—has gone. Schools, religious communities, and parish churches relentlessly diminish. The alienation of women heightens. The American episcopate itself appears significantly weakened in the quality and credibility of its leadership over these decades.

These negatives are not the whole story perhaps, but they do constitute an important part of the whole story. They infect the hope and enthusiasm with which Catholics live, work, and possess a sense of themselves. The church in the United States appears in retreat, and lives with an increasing sense of diminishment, threat, incapacity, and sterility. To recognize all this cumulative negativity is not to succumb to its rhetorical exaggeration. But despite the astonishing popularity of the present pope and the hope placed in his government, one cannot escape the fact that among Christian denominations in the United States, Catholicism has registered the greatest proportion of those who have abandoned their Christian denominations.[1]

This dark experience settles for many Christians upon their own interior battles: with the fears and uncertainties that are the struggles of their solitude, the frustrations of their expectations, the sensed inability to pray or to achieve any significantly supportive religious meaning, the sterility of the preaching they are offered, the unsettling disappointment with themselves and with others, the banality and often dull and progressive failure of their marriages and their families in divorce. Institutional and creedal collapses reinforce this sinking weakness and aloneness. Catholics, as well as ex-Catholics, can also discover in bitterness that life has become cruel and that early promises have withered. The religious beliefs they once held may still be given a generic and abstract adherence, but now they are found to make no difference in their thoughts and in their loves. What may have once been a steady practice of prayer and familiarity with God has become the experience of emptiness, the cruel realization that "You've changed the rules of the game."

And into the darkness of these worlds in which so much seems lost or threatened or sterile, comes the challenging question of Jesus to the once-blind beggar in the ninth chapter of John: "Do you believe in the Son of Man?"

---

1. Lydia Saad, "Churchgoing among U.S. Catholics Slides to Tie Protestants," *Gallup*, April 9, 2009. *Gallup* registered the following: "According to Gallup Poll trends on church attendance among American Christians, weekly attendance among Protestants has been fairly steady over the past six decades, averaging 42% in 1955 versus 45% in the middle of the current decade. However, attendance among Roman Catholics dropped from 75% to 45% over the same period."

A Surrender That Is a Triumph

This is one of the most searching questions with which the Johannine Jesus confronts human beings. One can never feel as alone as when attempting to engage it honestly—as did this blind beggar. There is the descent into a progressive loneliness as he attempts to remain faithful to what has visited his life. Notice how his abandonment gathers force through this chapter. He was first taken by his neighbors to the authorities, then deserted by his own parents in their terror, and finally turned out by the religious leaders of his people. He is now utterly alone—he has lost everything—and yet has remained in faithful honesty to the One he cannot name.

And into his solitude Jesus comes once more. In fact, the Scripture is more poignant and moving. It says that Jesus "found him" (*heuron auton*)—in the same way as the shepherd would find the lost sheep (Luke 15:3–7); as the frantic woman would find the lost coin (Luke 15:8–9); as Paul would pray in Philippians that he might be "found" in Christ (Phil. 3:9). At the very moment the beggar has lost everything, yet he has been found by the One he cannot yet name. Only then can the searching last question of his rebirth be placed: "Do you believe in the Son of Man?" What a question to put to someone who has nothing!

For the question embodies the judgment of God—what John calls the *krima* of God that Jesus is. Right after the cured man's final confession, Jesus summarizes his whole life through this poignant event: "For judgment I came into this world, that those who do not see may see, and that those who see may become blind" (John 9:39). The judgment of Jesus involves such an utter reversal of human expectations that those who take this question seriously come to live in a world of religious mystery, awe, and even contradictions.[2] The questions of Jesus lead one to the judgment of God.

---

2. Raymond Brown, SS, *The Gospel according to John: I–XII*, Anchor Bible (Garden City, NY: Doubleday, 1966), 376–77.

Granted the profound reach of the question, what does it mean? How does it tell comprehensively upon human life—tell in such a paradoxical way that it actually becomes part of the "good news"? What does Jesus's questioning ask from this man, and from all human beings, and from those who hear this Gospel?

He frames his question with the phrase *pistuein eis*: "To believe in." This phrase is almost uniquely Johannine. It is found only once in Matthew (18:6), while being present thirty-one times in John. What does it mean in John? Why is it introduced here?

This phrase denotes the turn, the absolute revolution, needed for eternal life. It gives the actual reason for the incarnation: "God so loved the world that he gave his only Son, that whoever *believes in him* should not perish but have eternal life" (John 3:16; cf. 11:25). To believe in Jesus in this way is to reverse any ultimate dependence or expectations upon the world for one's meaning. It allows one to receive the Spirit of God with a new freedom: "Now this he said about the Spirit, which those who *believed in him* were to receive" (7:39). It catches up in its promise all the longings of human beings that death would not be the last word in their lives: "Whoever lives and *believes in me* shall never die" (11:26). It is the final and definitive promise and mystery into which Jesus incorporates his disciples: "Let not your hearts be troubled; you believe in God, *believe also in me*" (14:1). Then what does this mean, "to believe in him"? What is the disciple of Jesus summoned to?

In the grace of his promise, it summons human beings to give themselves over, to commit themselves absolutely to him; to entrust him utterly with their lives. This is the surrender that is paradoxically a triumph. "To believe in him" is to say from the depths of human conviction that Jesus is Lord. In utter trust and love one hands one's life over to Jesus. This is the initial revolution contained in the question of Jesus.

Look how the blind man comes into this question. He was led through successive stages, finally to be transformed by Jesus. One can watch this religious development as his story unfolds—as he answers, even at great personal sacrifice, the advancing questioning of others. To the neighbors' question, he identified the One who had healed him as "the man called Jesus" (John 9:11). To the Pharisees he replied: "He is a prophet" (9:17). To the religious authorities his answer was: he is a man "from God" (9:33). Only after all this does the climactic question come: "Do you believe in the Son of Man?" (9:35)—the eschatological bearer of final salvation— the hope of the world, who transforms the world by definitively fulfilling its destiny and longings, and the One whom even the beggar consequently can worship and trust.

Rudolf Bultmann[3] traces the emergence and growth of grace in this man's life: The healed man has recognized Jesus as a prophet (9:17), as authorized by God (9:33), and thus has come as far as he can within the Jewish sphere. But as yet he is unaware that his helper is the "Son of Man," the eschatological bringer of salvation. He does not know that, if he wants to see Jesus as he really is, he must leave the old sphere completely behind him. Any man who is basically honest and upon whom Jesus has made an impression can come as far as he has come. But the decisive step only arrives when the question is put explicitly, when a man is confronted by the self-revelation in the world (9:38).

And at this moment, this is what Jesus is doing. He has himself become the question. But how is it even possible for the beggar to hear the question that is Jesus, after so many years of sorrow and discouragement? Subjective condition is his purity of heart—a faithful honesty about his own experience: the undeviating determination to live authentically by the truth insofar as it disclosed itself to this poor and wretched man. The beggar faithfully described to his neighbors what had happened. The beggar "did the truth" as this reached and claimed him, and "those who do what is true

3. Rudolf Bultmann, *The Gospel of John: A Commentary,* trans. G. R. Beasley-Murray, R. W. N. Hoare, and J. K. Riches (Philadelphia: Westminster, 1971), 338–39.

come to the light" (John 3:21 NRSV). These remain the conditions for any authentic religious faith.

When John Henry Newman fell ill at Leonforte in Sicily and was ridden with fever, the realization of his being faithful to the directions of his conscience, to the truth as he knew it, was steady in its support. "Yet still I said to myself, I have not sinned against the light."[4] In this Gospel narrative, the blind man clings to the truth, a truth that enters his life as a question, the question posed by everything around him. The blind man was faithful, truthful, even when his parents deserted him. He was doggedly honest with the Pharisees—despite threats. He was uncompromisingly governed by the truth as it came into his life. Now this fidelity made him able to hear the final question: Will you entrust your life to Jesus, the Son of Man? Will you trust him with the life that allegiance to the truth has gradually purified? "Do you believe in the Son of Man?"

In many ways, the pattern and the progress in the contemporary church must be similar. Death and dying, obduracy and blindness, arrogance and ignorance can seem almost universal, but redemptive grace reduplicates in its remarkable paradoxes so much of the history of this beggar—each time at a different depth and in a different pattern. The call to remain faithful to the truth, despite the repudiation and contempt of others, remains stern and demanding. The beggar gradually and irremediably lost everything. He gave it over for the truth as it revealed itself to him, as it grasped him. This enabled him not so much to find Jesus, but to be found by him, to have Jesus find him, to speak to him (9:35) and to call him.

Jesus asks: Now will you go further? You have been true to the light you know, and in spite of everything, you have been faithful to what calls to your conscience. Now will you commit yourself to the

---

4. John Henry Cardinal Newman, *Apologia Pro Vita Sua*, ed. Martin J. Svaglic (Oxford: Clarendon, 1967), 43. Cf. Meriol Trevor, *Newman: The Pillar of the Cloud* (London: Macmillan, 1962), 131.

mystery that you do not comprehend while so many of the things you have relied upon up to this time fail you? For finally here, you are not so much to comprehend the mystery, but the mystery is to comprehend you. Does your fidelity to truth extend that far? In Bultmann's words, this is to leave the old sphere behind. Does the truth bring you to this revolution in your fidelity? Does fidelity confirm you in your trust?

In all this history and in all this sorrow, such an unyielding commitment to the truth will demand a trust in the One the beggar has seen and who is speaking to him (9:37). All of this has become the question: Has the claim of truth become absolute in your life? Inextricably, the absolute commitment to truth, if the faith is to be authentic, is the condition for the possibility of faith.[5] Only in this way is death "swallowed up in victory" (1 Cor. 15:54), in an uncompromising commitment that is appropriate only to the presence and truth of God.

---

5. For a further delineation, see Michael J. Buckley, SJ, "The Negation of Atheism," in *Denying and Disclosing God: The Ambiguous Progress of Modern Atheism* (New Haven: Yale University Press, 2004), 120–38.

⁀⟨ 4 ⟩⟊

"HOW CAN YOU BELIEVE?"

*"I do not receive glory from men. But I know
that you have not the love of God within you.
I have come in my Father's name, and you do
not receive me; if another comes in his own
name, him you will receive. How can you believe, who receive glory from one another and
do not seek the glory that comes from the only
God?"* (John 5:41–44)

The Absolute Character of Faith

This question of preeminent grace presses relentlessly on the central condition for any religious inquiry into the Gospel of John—an
inquiry darkened by the clamor of contradictory etiologies and
professions, ranging from exemplar to fraud. While the entire Gospel sets as its actual and governing challenge the question "Do you
believe in the Son of Man?" (9:35), here the question centers more
directly upon the fundamental possibilities and conditions for an
absolute faith in Jesus: "How can you believe?"

The Gospel questions how anyone can subscribe to the staggering words, actions, or claims of this historically limited and

particular person. At this moment, every Christian is examined for the possibilities of a commitment of faith to Jesus. The Christian is never more *contra mundum* than when called upon to answer for the possibilities of such absolute faith in the Son of Man. On what possible grounds can anyone honestly come to such an unconditional affirmation in a human being?

In much contemporary culture, a conviction of this dimension is easily dismissed as illusion, its falsity to emerge in times of pressure, alienation, disappointment, or personal anguish. Do not persistent, haunting doubts indicate that fiction is here, a basic self-deception? Generation after generation have discovered "cultural faith" to be inadequate, hopelessly frail before social experience. Sigmund Freud's judgment is harshly negative: "In other matters [than religion] no sensible person will behave so irresponsibly or risk contempt with such feeble grounds for his opinions and for the line he takes. It is only in the highest and most sacred things that he allows himself to do so. . . . Where questions of religion are concerned, people are guilty of every sort of dishonesty and intellectual misdemeanor."[1] The history of Western culture demonstrates that in no other area is self-deception or illusion so possible, so prevalent, and so emotionally fostered as in religious fanatical belief or faith. The patently insubstantial or hysterical character of much emotionally charged— not to say overwrought—religious argument and of such unfounded beliefs has fatally undermined their social credibility.

Human beings may urgently persuade themselves, however, that their "faith" is solidly founded and irrefragable, that in unquestionable creedal affirmations, social consensus, and moral practices they have secured an entrustment and obtained a certitude about their beliefs, as indeed about their "faith," that must be without question. Such a certitude, however, has often revealed itself under pressure to be chimerical. When one strips away all fatuous reassurances from what is actually disclosed, what is left?

---

1. Sigmund Freud, *The Future of an Illusion* (New York: Norton, 1961), 32.

What does one find oneself really committed to? What is actually uncovered by a process of demanding and rigorously honest observation to be the actual object of religious faith? Illusion, even to the point of absurdity, is so pervasive here. So recognizable is the underlying strong wish fulfillment driven by the unconscious desire for the total security of human life in the face of death.

Faith in the understanding of John's Gospel engages something absolute and simply nonnegotiable, the foundation of all other negotiations, a commitment to which everything else is relative. Has the psalmist not insisted upon the absolute character of this conviction?

> For God alone my soul waits in silence,
>> for my hope is from him.
> He only is my rock and my salvation,
>> my fortress; I shall not be shaken.
> On God rests my deliverance and my honor;
>> my mighty rock, my refuge is God.
> Trust in him at all times, O people;
>> pour out your heart before him;
> God is a refuge for us. (Ps. 62:5–8)

This is breathtaking in the strength of its claim: "For God alone." Alone. Faith's final independence from anything finite or idolatrous is a demand upon the religious faithful, the demand that nothing, in Saint Benedict's words, is to be preferred to the love of God.[2] In faith God is reverenced as Absolute, before which every other human claim and protestation is relativized. That is why the Gospel of John roots the inability to believe in the failure to love God. When is such an absolute in evidence in human experience? Is it not a chimera?

---

2. Benedict of Nursia, *Rule of Benedict*, ed. and trans. Bruce L. Venarde (Cambridge, MA: Harvard University Press, 2011), 33.

Quite honestly, does the usual religious belief in our culture, our churches, and our theology, even within the social fabric of the church, exhibit anything of such a stark and absolute feature? Does bourgeois, "adjusted" Christianity embody or witness this kind of faith? So the question rises judgmentally out of John's Gospel: Is this what I am to you? Is there actually a "glory" that in contemporary religious experience comes only from the one God and is the foundation of belief? Or is the interpretation of Jesus diagnostically more accurate: "You do not receive me?" Does belief exist anywhere? And this gives rise to the trenchant question that is unavoidable in the Gospels: "When the Son of man comes, will he find faith on earth?" (Luke 18:8). Is such an absolute faith actual? Will it ever be actual?

Prestige, God, and the Acclaim That Comes from Others

Jesus says nothing to soften his question. It occurs in the fifth chapter of John, long before the ninth chapter and the blind beggar. It emerges during a great confrontation with the Pharisees. This terrible question is addressed to the Pharisees: "How can you believe, who receive glory from one another and do not seek the glory that comes from the only God?" (John 5:44).

"How can you believe?" Christian faith or belief is always a victory over the world. Faith is always "in spite of." But more importantly, it is contingent upon accepting the glory that is from Jesus, upon receiving the experience that alone makes it possible for one to possess faith. The Christian answer to the question "how is it possible to believe?" is Jesus Christ.

There may be—and certainly are—other ways of coming to belief. But the final signature and sign of Christian faith is the influence of Jesus. Faith is not only the gift of Jesus but also the culminating victory of his Spirit over the world. For Jesus is both the object of faith and the motive for faith. It is he that makes faith both possible and actual. Only the courage that comes from the steady influence of Jesus makes it possible to deny the skepticisms and cynicisms that mark the presence of the "world" in human consciousness and convictions and render it impossible to believe. For religion is not enough. Religion is not the same thing as faith.

One mistakes this question badly unless one recognizes that the Pharisees to whom it was put were the "good people," the authoritatively zealous people of the time. The priestly caste stood corrupted by power, money, social adjustment, and political compromise. The Pharisees, in contrast, remained unyieldingly faithful to the Torah and to the commitments of Israel itself in spite of all. They were unashamedly and professedly religious, living rigorously and without compromise. They were honored by the people for this religious dedication. They enjoyed enormous prestige. This was to constitute the glory they received.

Their place in this heightened reverence of the people—their religious repute—gave to many of them a feeling of religious entitlement, a sensibility that carried with it an incorrigible self-righteousness: an expectation that theirs was the first place; theirs was the doctrine that others would and should follow. The people needed no other influence to shape their opinions. In the concrete this devolved into the contempt in which they held so many others. They exhibited a harshness in condemning and dismissing others. This expectation of honor and deference as well as the arrogance with which they dismissed others—this pride—Jesus says, made belief in him impossible. It could not sustain the openness and devotion that Jesus necessitated.

This self-assuredness calls easily to mind Duns Scotus's description of the terrible sin of the angels. Scotus maintained that the superlative angelic intellect in its anticipation grasped something of the divine plan of salvation. The angels saw that the divine would assume humanity. They saw in the incarnation a human being who in the person of Jesus was united with the divine. But many of them, conscious of their vast superiority over anything human, found it impossible to reverence as God one who in station and nature was so much their inferior, so obviously beneath them, namely, Jesus. Their attitude drew them inescapably to despise Jesus as inferior. Thus from the cancerous contemplation of their own excellence, they progressed into a pride that issued in the contempt in which they held others—and from this to all other sins.

For some Pharisees in the Gospel of Luke, the honor they expected and upon which they had come addictively to depend spelled out a total repugnance toward believing in the presence of God united with something so obviously and hopelessly inferior—an itinerant carpenter-teacher with a hick Galilean accent, surrounded by these enthusiastic yahoos from the hill country. To reverence or defer to such a one in any absolute way would be patently absurd. That their own place would yield to this displacement, to this humiliation, was even more absurd. It would be to debase the sacred that they were created to mirror and strengthen. Hence, in the midst of the massive conflicts of John's fifth chapter, Jesus asks them this question—which can carry such relevance today and which can be either warning or diagnosis for anyone considering the possibility of authentic faith—"faith in spite of." From the cross to the contemporary church, faith can entail in its love and its reverence the profound experience of the hiddenness of glory, of profound failure and disappointment. To demand the alternative is simply to court disbelief.

"How can you believe, who receive glory from one another and do not seek the glory that comes from the only God?" (John 5:44).

It is out of this contradiction that Ignatius of Loyola builds his classic "Principle and Foundation": There is one Absolute, and this is the reality of God. The choice of everything else—whether success or failure—is to be evaluated as it embodies and advances the glory of God. Everything else is finally relative; the only absolute is "the glory that comes from the one God." And so Ignatius writes: "[The human person] was created to praise, reverence, and serve God our Lord, and in this way [*mediante isto*] to save their soul. And the other things on the face of the earth were created for the sake of the human person, and to help them in following out the end for which they were created. Hence it follows that human beings should make use of creatures insofar as they help them in this end and should withdraw from them insofar as they are a hindrance."[3]

This conviction lies at the heart and "in-forms" the Christian insistence on detachment or indifference—not the Stoic *apatheia*, but an uncompromising option for the glory of God that alone gives context, weight, perduring meaning, and ultimate value to all other loves. The glory that comes from finite things makes eternal sense here only within the glory that comes from God. This should never mean that one loves things less. On the contrary, one loves them more, and more authentically loves them as they exist. That is how God loves them. Human beings are called to love them, as they actually are. The love of God does not mitigate but increases the love for the creation that he has given. God is the source of their creation—not in competition with it. It would be distortion and blasphemy to assert that God is in competition with his creation.

One does not advance the obedience, love, and reverence of God by despising the things he has created and loved and given to those he loves and through which he has manifested himself and given himself to those he created. This is the glory of God. Creation reaches this pitch as one comes to understand the glory of God manifested in all things.

For God is always present, but when that presence reaches an intensity of human experience, one speaks not so much of the presence of God as of the glory of God. The glory of God is the palpable manifestation of the reality of God.

This is crucially important. For one does not advance in the

---

3. Ignatius of Loyola, "Principle and Foundation," in *The Spiritual Exercises*, trans. J. Rickaby, SJ (London: Burns, Oates and Washbourne, 1936), 18. Note that *hombre* in the Spanish has been translated so that it refers not to the masculine specifically, but to the more generic human person.

love of God by despising the things that he has created and loved and given to those he loves. And thus in John's Gospel, the glory that comes from God is primordial and definitive. In the universe of creatures, everything else takes upon itself a holiness as it bespeaks the glory that comes from God. Removed from that context, everything can disintegrate into violence and cancerous distortion.

The Temptation of Glory

In T. S. Eliot's play *Murder in the Cathedral*, Thomas à Beckett is subjected to a series of temptations. The final one—the seduction that came so subtly that it alone took him by surprise—he came to recognize only over time. It encouraged him to do all the good that he was doing; to undergo the pain that he would suffer; to remain resolute about the rights of the church; to resist the opposition from disloyal bishops; to remain independent before the interventions of the monarch and the plotting of political powers; and so to go to his death as a martyr. This was everything he believed he should do. But it urged him to do all this because of the respect and admiration this would bring to his name forever, an enhanced public appreciation of his worth, the glory of endless adulation and approval. Only gradually did he come to distinguish temptation from grace.

Thomas was initially tempted by the very course he must choose, by the very life he must live, just as the Pharisees were tempted by loyalty to the law. He was not tempted to deny his mission and the apostolic witness of his life. He was called to its total perversion, to have it twisted to the glory that comes from human beings. Only gradually did he come to see the profound evil under this apparent good, to understand that evil mostly comes corrosively into the good person's life not as evil but under the appearance of good. The temptations of the good person, the lure into evil, are above all matters of deception, disordered appetite, and the appearance of good:

> Now is my way clear, now is the meaning plain:
> Temptation shall not come in this kind again.
> The last temptation is the greatest treason:
> To do the right deed for the wrong reason. . . .
> For those who serve the greater cause
> May make the cause serve them.[4]

It all lies in a definitional shift of motivation. This new specification of appetite is as subtle and unsuspected as it is profound and corrupting. The good that human beings are charged to do mutates from an organic growth to emerge cancerous, corrupted beyond its native character, arrogant, destructive of all religious life, imprisoning, a *corruptio boni*: the great secret of evil. We can see this not only in others, but also in ourselves. The things that are good can become twisted into evil. Acts of deference and humility can minister to personal advancement through the approval they evoke. The strident rigorism within any religious community, within a cause, or within a Catholic culture can mask a deeper violence, a pervasive judgmental contempt for the religiously inferior and socially compromised. A serious commitment to taxing work can disguise a hidden, but insatiable, expectation for recognition or security or for some other form of power over others.

Deception under the appearance of good is insatiable. Projects may be undertaken, but when enthusiastic public approval is not subsequently forthcoming, the project dies in bitterness and in raucous claims about the indifference of others, especially those in authority. The actual motivation gradually emerges, indicated

---

4. T. S. Eliot, *Murder in the Cathedral*, in *The Complete Poems and Plays, 1909–1950* (San Diego: Harcourt, Brace & Co., 1971), 196.

by the spirit it fathers. At its initiation, the work itself may be good, but the spirit in which it is carried out progressively corrupts and stains it, revealing its underlying dynamic. One often comes to know the real motivation undergirding salutary commitments and projects—not so much at their enthusiastic initiation, but as they course through time to reach their conclusion. If the beginning, middle, and end of the project bespeak the love, joy, peace, patience, and other marks of the Spirit, then the Galatians would recognize it is of God (Gal. 5:16–26). But if a project or commitment becomes characterized by bitterness, dishonesty, or unfairness, then it bears the sure signs of the absence of the Spirit either in whole or in part. Thus the history of the church and of all religious communities within the church indicates the inescapable need for the serious and objective discernment of spirits, an accurate reading of the "glory" that is being sought. The apparent good is not self-justifying. Friendships and commitments of many years can fall apart.[5]

For, in a thousand ways, "those who serve the greater cause / may make the cause serve them."[6] This can be enormously subtle. Sometimes a nuance at the initial formulation of an action or of a life can work the unexpected twist, the unrealized but profound reorientation so that zeal masks a hidden but vicious ambition; it is hidden because ambition and zeal, however profoundly contradictory, can look initially so much alike. The desire to get something achieved can mix the intrinsic worth of the project with the reflected glory of the accomplishment. A religious commitment that begins in self-denial can slip almost imperceptibly into an abiding or even demanding sense of entitlement—always present, easily wounded. The "religious" gradually slips away into the bitterness that manifests the perversion in motivation that has taken place.

---

5. Cf. the rules for discernment of spirits during the second week of the *Spiritual Exercises* of Saint Ignatius.

6. Eliot, *Murder in the Cathedral*, 196.

To use the gospel or the church, or even the religious needs of others, to enhance personal importance again carries infallibly a subtle sense of destructive self-entitlement and deception.

For all significant religious accomplishments, then, "seeking the glory that comes from human beings" paradoxically can constitute a continual temptation. One can come to depend instinctively upon deference and respect. This dependence, in turn, can poison religious existence, instrumentalizing this commitment to satisfy the sense of one's own achievements or one's own power or one's own respect in the eyes of others. As time passes, one can come to rely addictively upon these signs of prestige. They become like unwanted injections of morphine—a social deference or recognition even when it was not initially desired or sought after—but they become sharply and darkly missed as time passes and they are not forthcoming. One can subtly or not so subtly brag about previous accomplishments in order to evoke their now faded remains. One can resent it darkly when accomplishments or position is not remembered and recognized.

This dependence upon "the glory that comes from others," upon the positions and recognition and deference in daily life that bespeak personal prestige—Jesus says makes "belief in" him impossible. One has resolutely or compulsively lodged one's own security and sense of value elsewhere—given them over in a thousand ways to other human beings. One does what pleases or recommends or secures the favor of the people who count.

It can seem so slight, but it is in this context that the question of Jesus to the externally religious of his time takes on a particular poignancy. This question of Jesus is about motivations and support systems for those who have instrumentalized the manifold good that they do to reassurances about their own worth. This is all about what makes faith possible or impossible, and hence the question of Jesus: "How can you believe, who receive glory from one another and do not seek the glory that comes from the only God?"

⑸

"SIMON, SON OF JOHN, DO YOU LOVE ME?"

When they had finished breakfast, Jesus said to Simon Peter, "Simon, son of John, do you love me more than these?" He said to him, "Yes, Lord; you know that I love you." He said to him, "Feed my lambs." A second time he said to him, "Simon, son of John, do you love me?" He said to him, "Yes, Lord; you know that I love you." He said to him, "Tend my sheep." (John 21:15–16)

Appetite for Achievement

A strange cast of darkness can settle upon lives given generously to the service of others. Crowding out prior enthusiasms and even the evocative attraction of the Gospels, this darkness can over time stifle spontaneous generosity and the idealism that lies at its heart. It can easily settle upon and dissipate the forms of human dedication— whether academic studies, professional commitments, or prolonged public service. It does not so much bear upon conscious thoughts as upon circumambient feelings and a sense of purpose. One cannot see what was previously a light for decisions and choice.

A strong, compulsive demand to "get ahead," for example, can fuel a real struggle for a confirmation of worth by surpassing others. In this unarticulated competition, "others" gradually become the unrecognized enemy, the silent ones to whom one must prove oneself. This darkness always carries a strong sense of anger and frustration, of demanding strategies to "make it" or to measure up for inadequacies.

In this experience, one gradually becomes liable to the cancerous, destructive exaggeration of slights, taken to be of enormous, distorted importance, even though if admittedly of little weight. Trivial or negative remarks are received as inadvertent "disclosures" of what people "really think." One obsesses over criticisms or falls prey to easy feelings of guilt or becomes enraged if one's competency or intentions are somehow faulted. These slights may appear embarrassingly trivial or small, little things, but in their own hidden way they sear. Human beings can focus so much of life around the recognition of deference expected or owed, the denial of which gives way to a great sense of emptiness—an emptiness where there should have been a certain pride of place. Even great enterprises and great men have been torpedoed by absurd and frustrated expectations.

Under one guise or another, people may restlessly struggle to counter a sense of inadequacy, to prove themselves by notable accomplishments, even religious ones. Like the extrinsically evaluated child of Psychology 101, they may possess the smile or the dedication that can charm all—a "ready" personality—but they are really quite careful. Everything becomes "ratings." Popularity, "grades" in one form or another, and acknowledgments carry unspoken importance—even if at enormous cost. Much is dependent upon praise and prestige, the sense of being publicly approved. But it is never quite enough. What is possessed is taken as acknowledgment of one's accomplishments but not of oneself. One repeats the endless, futile labors of Sisyphus—struggling with great effort to get the massive rock securely up the hill, but once it is on the top, the lumbering boulder inexorably rolls back down. Sisyphus, in whatever human form, must always begin over again, dogged by guilt, frustration, emptiness, or by an insatiable perfectionism, urged into his emptiness by the groups or the ideals with which he yearns to be associated. His is a weary and tormented life.

This insatiable appetite even for religious achievements, including in ministry to others, and for the praise that serves as its public confirmation manifests itself in the most paradoxical of fashions. Perhaps the most striking is the consistent and enervating inability to forgive, either oneself or another. One can never accept in some transformational way the forgiveness of one's own sins, because one cannot forgive oneself for being who one is.[1]

Failure and Forgiveness

There is something of this in all human beings, but that is not the point of this scene from the Gospel of John. This is not the end of the story. Is there any opportunity for a humane and balanced resolution of this contradiction? Is there any way in which a person can emerge out of this darkness? Is there any way a human being can come to peace with what he or she is and with the limitations of what he or she has accomplished?

Paradoxically, peace can flow into such a human life through the strange confluence of two events: First, if such a person actually fails—suffers rank, undeniable failure, either because the person did not meet obvious and serious responsibilities or because real, undisguisable faults in the person's character and competence resulted in embarrassing failure. This is to suggest the contradictory, but profound, value classically associated in Christian spir-

1. See Michael J. Buckley, SJ, "Because Beset with Weakness . . . ," in *To Be a Priest: Perspectives on Vocation and Ordination*, ed. Robert E. Terwilliger and Urban T. Holmes (New York: Seabury, 1975), 125–30.

ituality with humiliations. They dislodge a false sense of self in the interest of authenticity. They can usher in a renewed and vital sense of honest integrity.

Second, at that moment or after it has passed and one lives with the shame of memories, there is a chance for the radical transformation of this experience—if someone will accept and love the person as the person is found, as he or she really is, without pretense. This is to redeem, not to excuse, for love can transform humiliations. Now at the moment of humiliation, there is no ready experience of achievements that are buying anything. The person is embarrassed, overwhelmed, and humbled. There is no immediate sense of accomplishment or worth. The transformation of this failure can only occur if someone will actually reach out to the person in love—in an action that was not in any way "bought." It is an action that is free and could have been omitted. Through this affirmation the person's own value is affirmed and love is experienced, and experienced as unmerited, unbought, unconditioned, and undeniable.

This gratuitous love of others for the person, which has not been merited or bought, has been visited like grace upon him or her. Only in this context can one understand what the forgiveness of sins means in Christianity and why it is placed at the summit of God's dealings with human beings. For this is how God forgives sins. Forgiveness is the gift in love by the renewed and definitional spirit of God within the soul. Forgiveness is thus quite simply God's gift of himself. Let us look once more at this culmination of divine goodness, taken at the starkest point of its denial.

A shameful failure or a series of such failures may have been occasioned either by a conscious choice of evil or by the neglect in one of a thousand ways of the good that exists as a specification and as an obligation in one's life. In so many such choices, consciously or implicitly, a human being may either accept or exclude the influence of God within his or her life, loves, or consciousness. This exclusion of God is what has been termed metaphorically a "turning away from God." And this turning away is of the essence of sin, the actual or the habitual exclusion of the influence and presence of God from human life.

Then, at that juncture, let such a person experience deeply in some mysterious way that God actually loves the person, is calling to the person, offering to accept him or her as his loved son or daughter in a love that cannot be turned aside. God is always present as an offer, irrespective of what the person has chosen. Only in this way does one have some experience of sin and of what constitutes the forgiveness of sins.

Sin is the chosen absence of God, an absence chosen by human beings. The forgiveness of sins is not some fictitious pretense that what happened did not happen, or that what has been rejected has not been rejected. The forgiveness of sins is not an alibi nor an elaborate excuse in a quest for self-justification. The forgiveness of sins engages the recognition of evil, of some conscious and chosen absence of the goodness of God. Forgiveness takes place through the gift of the renewed and definitional presence of God within the soul. The forgiveness of sins in its profoundest meaning is God's gift of himself. God forgives sins by flooding with his presence that absence that human beings may have chosen. God forgives sins by giving himself to us once more. Forgiveness of sins is the insistent and transforming presence of God in lives that have affectively and deliberately excluded his grace as a determining presence. Despite how profoundly counterintuitive this is, then, the forgiveness of sins may well be the highest human experience of the unconditioned, unmerited love of God. And this is the meaning and the reach of the questions of Jesus to Peter.

Peter and Forgiveness

The reason the questions of the twenty-first chapter are so poignant and so endlessly meaningful is that Peter has become paradigmatic of all human beings. Peter is Everyman. The shame of the bombast and failure is still with him. His triple denial was predicted by Jesus in the face of his empty protestations of faithfulness to death (John 13:38). In a certain naïve arrogance, he had boasted of his endless fidelity in contrast to the faithlessness of others. During the trial before the high priest, his denials followed hard on the heels of his boast (18:17, 25, 27). Peter is really an easy figure to analyze and dismiss—the *New Yorker* could do it in a paragraph: "Volatile, over-eager, hides fearfulness under pomposity; self-promoting, boasting; the hiatus between his words and his performance is enormous; basically, an inflated and absurd figure."

But Jesus loved Peter. When Peter arrogated power and importance to himself, Jesus corrected him. When Peter boasted before others, Jesus warned him. When Peter sinned, Jesus forgave him.

Notice again *how* Jesus forgives him—what the forgiveness of sins actually means in the Gospel of John, and has come to mean pervasively in Christian life. Jesus does not deny what has occurred—by saying, "Let's just pretend that it never happened"— or, as if human beings could be saved by pretense and unreality. Nor does Jesus trivialize Peter's denial by saying that the past is unimportant. On the contrary, the triple questions of Jesus parallel and recall the triple denial. The past is operatively present—even structurally emphasized. Nor does Jesus excuse it away: "I knew you weren't yourself, Peter." There is no excuse; that is the reason why the church remembers it now as forgiveness of sins, not their alibi. You excuse the excusable; you forgive the inexcusable. Nor does Jesus say to Peter, as he had to others, that his sins are forgiven, for that would have generalized what was very immediate and very personal. Jesus does not even tell Peter that he loves him.

What Jesus does is ask Peter for *his* love. Three times, Jesus makes it obvious that Peter's love means so much to him. He asks him for it—as a friend would ask a friend for confirmation of a friendship that he treasures and has broken. Peter means so much to Jesus that he asks Peter to confirm their friendship in spite of everything. This unmerited love is the strongest possible assertion of Peter's meaning and irreplaceable value to Jesus. It is the restoration of a friendship; it is even creative of a new goodness, as a person is changed by friendship and love.

How does Peter receive the questions of Jesus? How does he answer these questions? He does not directly protest his love—he has protested many things in the past, and these protestations have died in their attempt. What he does insist upon, what he has confidence in above anything else he could appeal to, is the intimate and comprehensive knowledge that Jesus has of him:

> "Lord, you know that I love you."
> "Lord, you know that I love you."
> "Lord, you know all things—
>   you know that I love you."

Peter can accept forgiveness in this loving knowledge that Jesus has of him—Jesus who knows all things and has loved him. This knowledge that Jesus has of him does not paralyze him. It empowers him. It is like the gaze of Jesus in that first moment of encounter by the Jordan. The knowledge is in Jesus's gaze upon him, in his reading Peter from within, with all the compassion that his knowledge makes possible. Peter can accept his forgiveness. The questions of Jesus meet with this repeated, humble, but deeply devoted "Lord, you know . . ."

To be forgiven is then to live the Christian life in that knowledge and in that gratuitous love that is found in the gaze of Jesus—in the knowledge that Jesus has of us, in the knowledge that Jesus had at the moment of the first encounter. "For if our heart condemns us, God is greater than our heart, and knows all things" (1 John 3:20 NKJV). To accept the forgiveness of sins is to live habitually in the knowledge that even if there is or has been a vicious excision of goodness from our lives, God has continued faithfully to want us and to love us. As for Peter, so also for us: the forgiveness of sins is the restoration of presence and friendship. We experience the forgiveness of sins when we experience that God in Jesus is asking for our love, that our human friendship means that much to him.

> Set me as a seal upon your heart,
>   as a seal upon your arm;
>   for love is strong as death. (Song 8:6)

This is the question in which every Christian hears his or her own name: "Simon, son of John, do you love me?"

⑥

"HAVE I BEEN WITH YOU SO LONG, AND YET YOU DO NOT KNOW ME?"

Philip said to him, "Lord, show us the Father, and we shall be satisfied." Jesus said to him, "Have I been with you so long, and yet you do not know me, Philip? He who has seen me has seen the Father; how can you say, 'Show us the Father'? Do you not believe that I am in the Father and the Father in me?"
(John 14:8–10)

Jesus's Gentle Rebuke

Although the Gospels number Philip among the Twelve, only the Fourth Gospel maps out in any detail his character and its gradual development. It does so through four separate episodes, each of which brings the others to a greater extension and theological depth. This religious development of Philip bears a remarkable resemblance to the evolution of faith in the blind beggar of the ninth chapter. Appropriating Jesus's question to Philip thus can enable one to trace the culmination of what will become an authentic Christian spirituality. For one can find here again and again what it is to be caught up in the attraction, the influence, and the draw of Jesus of Nazareth.

The first question entails a gentle but mysterious rebuke to Philip. To what could Jesus refer when he says, "Have I been with you so long, and yet you do not know me?" What is this "knowledge," what is this "so long a time"? What bespeaks duration and continuity in time with Jesus, the person that he is? Philip has insistently asked for revelation. His religious longing, however, will be satisfied only by the disclosure of the Father in the mysterious nuance of Jesus. This is done in four stages.

Philip's "So Long a Time"

Philip makes his first appearance in the Gospel at the initiation of Jesus's public life. Jesus has been moving to gather his disciples. The previous day opened with Andrew and an unnamed disciple. As Jesus would eventually find the blind beggar, so at this moment Jesus would find Philip. In the Gospel of John, Philip numbers among Jesus's first discoveries. At that moment of initial encounter, Jesus says to Philip quite simply: "Follow me"—and that is enough. In fact, it is a beginning; as with Andrew, Philip's vocation turns into communion. He immediately finds Nathaniel—as he himself has been found by Jesus. He tells Nathaniel that they have found the Messiah. Nathaniel demurs—and Philip's response is complete, is exactly what all apostolic and even later religious witness will finally embody: "Come and see" (1:46). This invitation signals the beginning of a communion that would last "so long a time."

In the later events chronicled in the sixth chapter, it is to Philip that Jesus addresses the first question that would introduce the feeding of the multitudes: "How are we to buy bread, so that these people may eat?" (6:5). The question is a test, says the Evangelist. Philip would move beyond simple vocation, to vocation and mission. Now he is to be probed or tested for a greater realization of what he is to become, and is to discover what Jesus can be, what Jesus can do—feed five thousand. Again, this development of Philip's understanding is not on a path dissimilar from that of the blind beggar.

So close does Philip come to be associated with Jesus, that in the twelfth chapter, when the first Gentiles attempt to approach Jesus, they go to Philip: "Sir," they tell him, "we would like to see Jesus." Philip was once the mediator for Nathaniel; now he is the mediator for those sheep "that are not of this fold" (10:16). When Jesus learns that the Gentiles have come to see him in this way, he realizes that the hour that is to become the paschal mystery has finally arrived, the hour for him to be glorified, and in this way to manifest his reality, and so to draw all human beings to himself (12:32).

The vocation of Philip is paradigmatic: it runs its course in many ways signatory of every Christian vocation. One enters this strange and unexpected journey in stages. There is the initial experience of first and oblique attraction; this gives impetus as well as inspiration to the subsequent communication to others that rises almost spontaneously as one speaks out concerning what or whom one has come to admire and love. There is a moment for the special mystery of the providence of Jesus toward the people, a mystery that is beyond Philip's anticipation, but one that he will serve. And, finally, all these moments give that continual association with Jesus that allows others to approach Jesus ministerially through Philip. All this background tells in the question of Jesus: "Have I been with you so long, and yet you do not know me, Philip?" (14:9). "So long" extends the beginnings of the public life, over the years of companionship and discipleship, to emerge as the hour's realization. "Yet you do not know me." One can be very long with Jesus, as was Philip and indeed are many Christians, and still hear this question. But what does this question mean?

And Yet You Do Not Know Me

What does it mean to know someone? How much personal knowledge is needed to know a human being in a human relationship?

"Yet you do not know me." Philip has been with the Lord from his calling through months of subsequent witness. Such is their companionship that people can and do approach Philip with the same request in a thousand different ways: "Sir, we wish to see Jesus" (12:21). But Philip still does not know him.

In so many ways, this request of the Gentiles opens up to the most profound meaning of what it is to be a contemporary Christian, for this request leads into the question to Philip. To "know" Jesus is the desire that brings the Christian to contemplate the last scene of Jesus, the paschal mystery and the self-communication of God.

Knowing Jesus Is Knowing God

Jesus has just told his disciples that he is going away and that they know the way he is traveling. Thomas—again so typically—answers quite honestly that they know neither his destination nor the path he is traveling. Jesus compounds the mystery by identifying himself as the Way and the Truth and the Life. Jesus claims to be the Way, because he is the manner and the path—one could even say the "method"—by which one can approach God or by which God can approach human beings. Jesus is the Way that one becomes intimately familiar with God. He is also the Truth about this God—the self-disclosure of God. Finally, he is Life because union with him imparts God's self-giving life. When his disciples come to know him, they do not come to know about God, but they come to know God. When they see him, then, they see the Father disclosed in Jesus. In this mystery the Christian becomes familiar and united with God through Jesus.

For in knowing and loving Jesus, the disciples are knowing and loving God. To say that Jesus is divine, as the early councils of the church would teach in various ways, is to say that God gives himself in Jesus Christ. Philip has to learn this not as a proposition about Jesus, but as the deepest expressed reality of Jesus—an intimate knowledge of God is giving himself in Jesus. Jesus is the tangible and historical and dogmatic availability of God; hence, the revelation of God to human beings.

A series of very strong statements in this vein have preoccupied the teaching authority of the church in recent decades. Benedict XVI has expressed it this way in his encyclical *Deus Caritas Est*:

> Love of God and love of neighbor are thus inseparable, they form a single commandment. But both live from the love of God who has loved us first. No longer is it a question, then, of a "commandment" imposed from without and calling for the impossible, but rather of a freely-bestowed experience of love from within, a love which by its very nature must then be shared with others. Love grows through love. Love is "divine" because it comes from God and unites us to God; through this unifying process it makes us a "we" which transcends our divisions and makes us one, until in the end, God is "all in all" (*1 Corinthians* 15:28).[1]

This teaching is fundamental to all Christianity, but its very fundamentality has paradoxically encouraged some to dismiss it as banal, thus manifesting how little of this claim has been registered, how much it has been supplemented and replaced by enthusiastic homiletics, social exhortation, and textbook theology. Winston Churchill gave voice to this dismissal in his exasperated comment on Anthony Eden's rhetoric, complaining that Eden's threadbare speech had incorporated every cliché known to the English-speaking world except "God is love."[2]

1. Benedict XVI, *Deus Caritas Est*, Vatican website, December 25, 2005; http://www.vatican.va/holy_father/benedict_xvi/encyclicals/documents/hf_ben-xvi_enc_20051225_deus-caritas-est_en.html, paragraph 18 (accessed August 1, 2014).

2. Fred R. Shapiro, ed., *The Yale Book of Quotations* (New Haven: Yale University Press, 2006), 155.

Compare the stark evangelical and patristic urgency with that of the manuals or textbooks over the centuries on this same mystery. Since the seventeenth century, manuals dominated and set the tone for the dogmatic propositions that dealt with the absolute character of the divine reality. They claimed, as their history, to be modeled on the greatest of the scholastics, Thomas Aquinas. But in fact, how did they proceed?

The manuals could begin with the existence of God. If the influence of the *Summa Theologiae* was strong, they might infer the existence of God from the movement of things, or from a chain of causes, or from the contingent universe, etc., coming finally to God inferred as the pure act of being. From this they would proceed to demonstrate what God cannot be and, consequently, what alone can be truly said of him. From there, the manualists would discuss divine knowledge and love, providence and predestination. All of this without a word about the mysteries of Christ in the Gospels. These immediate demonstrations were admittedly philosophical, but they made the propositions of the reality and nature of God dependent upon the contingent universe. In this philosophic discussion, Jesus and the mysteries of Christ are simply ignored, bypassed, sectioned off to a part of manual theology. It is simply astonishing to recall that Jesus plays little role foundationally in demonstrations that purport to establish the reality and character of God.

In the subsequent tractate on the Trinity and what follows, how much did Jesus Christ or the mysteries of his life enter into the discussion? If one faithfully followed the manuals, virtually not at all. Rather, the student would take statements from Scripture and show that this God is triune—and from there discuss notions and processions and relations, etc. Did this removal or distancing of Jesus Christ from the investigative and definitive study of God not affect the way Catholics came to think theologically about God, about grace, about providence? Did it not also affect the horizon within which the church understood itself, as well as religious life, marriage, and the family?

That is a genuine question. I do not know the full answer, but I would not be surprised to discover that this method of procedure profoundly shaped the way Catholics came to think about all the great Christian realities. Certainly it contrasts strongly with the theology of the Eastern churches, which situates all theology within the Trinitarian reality of God. In the divine economy, God is first and foremost seen as Father, and from that flows God as Son and as Spirit.

Let us ask a second question—one the pope raises. If one proceeds in the manner of the manualist tradition, what is the first divine attribute—the first thing one could say about God, upon which all other attributes depend? It would be the divine simplicity—that God is in no way composed, that he is uncaused, transcendent, the pure act of being—and all this is demonstrated by considerations of the divine simplicity. This is not a question of which of these attributes is true of God. All are true of God. It is a question of what is primary and contextual in our considerations, what gives stability and color to everything else.

But if, in contrast, one comes to God through the person and life of Jesus of Nazareth and the experience of Christians in the grace of his presence and influence, and the primordial primacy of the personal in all theological reflections, what is the first attribute one would come to—what is the first thing one would say about God? For Benedict XVI it is the divine compassion.

These theological decisions about primacy are not simply abstract nuances in the study of theology. They bear upon the basis and structure of the human being's relationship with God and how the church fulfills the petition of Philip, "Show us the Father." These are central understandings, and they profoundly affect the content of one's relationship with God, even persons' relationships with one another and with the rest of the world. What happens to Christian people when the first rule by which one judges the church's members is not by how much they embody the divine transcendence or separation from the world, but by how much they embody the divine compassion—so that the ascetical and mystical dynamism and promise of the community are to be for its members a "school of charity"?

For what one thinks of Christian life depends radically (even if it is never articulated) on what one thinks of God—and that depends, according to Pope Benedict XVI, on what one thinks of Jesus Christ and how he is experienced in the graces of human life. God always specifies, or should specify, how one thinks theologically. If instead compassion—or divine love freely given to human beings—specifies the divine reality, this will give a radical character to the theology and the Christian life that eventuate.

If the theological reflections of the church had been centered over the past centuries on the compassion of God as the attribute of primary and determinative importance for human beings, if this had been central and unavoidable in any reflection on God, would such aberrations as have stained Catholic culture over the centuries and of which the church is presently so ashamed been possible: the repressions of the Inquisition, the enslavement of peoples, the burning of witches, the contempt for Jews and alien creeds, the harshness in judging other religions, the contempt for the religious persuasions of even alienated people? Each of these eventuated from some form of a profound failure: the failure to know God above all in his compassion.

Fyodor Dostoevsky insisted on the primacy of this call to compassion. It was of the essence of Jesus. In *The Brothers Karamazov*, Ivan Karamazov tells the story of "the Grand Inquisitor," a story that captures Dostoevsky's understanding of Christianity. The narrative opens when Christ returns to the world:

> In His infinite mercy He came once more among men in that human shape in which He walked among men for three years fifteen centuries ago. He came down to that "hot pavement" of the southern town [Seville] in which on the day before almost a hundred heretics had, *ad majorem Dei gloriam*, been burnt by

the cardinal, the Grand Inquisitor, in a magnificent *auto da fe*, in the presence of the king, the court, the knights, the cardinals, the most charming ladies of the court, and the whole population of Seville.

He came softly, unobserved, and yet, strange to say, every one recognized Him. That might be one of the best passages in the poem. I mean why they recognized Him. The people are irresistibly drawn to Him, they surround Him, they flock around Him, follow Him. He moves silently in their midst with a gentle smile of infinite compassion.[3]

How did they recognize Christ in Dostoevsky's parable? Because of his "infinite mercy," "the smile of infinite compassion." They knew Christ as God reaching out to human beings in limitless compassion. So is God and so are the things of God to be recognized. Compassion is the intelligibility of God.

Earlier in these considerations about the questions of Jesus, it was argued that the experience of the absolute claim of truth is the experience of God within human lives, as it was for the blind beggar. This claim realizes, as it embodies, the unconditioned sovereignty of God.

But human beings only know Jesus, Pope Benedict claims, and the God whom he discloses, when they recognize in him "God who is rich in mercy." The absolute, irrefragable knowledge of God occurs when one is configured to Jesus and to his compassion in such a way that one instinctively recognizes connaturally what he would accept, and further, what he would do and where his Spirit is at work.

Such a transformation of intelligence and affectivity is the work of the Spirit of Christ—poured forth into one's heart so that one would recognize him, know him, and become like him. One can

3. Fyodor Dostoevsky, *The Brothers Karamazov*, trans. Richard Pevear and Larissa Volokhonsky (New York: Knopf, 1992), 248–49.

recognize Christ, and God in Christ and what is of Christ, if one has been configured to Christ and so empowered to the discernment of spirits. Further, if one would judge the growth or the decline of authentic discipleship of Christian life, perhaps one would best look here: What is the quality or depth of compassion that marks these men and women? In their following of Christ, what is the reach of their community to embody that compassion? This is the kind of knowledge that obtains only when one becomes the one known. This is to fulfill the great prayer of Paul: "That I may know him and the power of his resurrection, and may share his sufferings, becoming like him in his death, that if possible I may attain the resurrection from the dead" (Phil. 3:10–11).

For the Christian, this is worth everything else—to come to know Jesus with this intimate knowledge, and to know God in Jesus Christ. For Christianity—and any form of Christian life itself—is much more like a friendship than it is like a philosophy of life or behavior. This knowledge was a passion for Saint Paul, writing to the church in Philippi: "But whatever gain I had, I counted as loss for the sake of Christ. Indeed I count everything as loss because of the surpassing worth of knowing Christ Jesus my Lord" (Phil. 3:7–8). This knowledge is a response to Philip's question and worth one's entire life. It lies behind Jesus's question to Philip, "Have I been with you so long, and yet you do not know me?"

∜(7)ᴗ

"WHAT IS THIS TO ME AND TO YOU?"

*When the wine gave out, the mother of Jesus
said to him, "They have no wine." And Jesus
said to her, "What is this to me and to you?"*
(John 2:3–4)

The Sacred Sign and Gift of Others

Let me assess the weight of this question of Jesus in a manner more
personal. While in Florence studying Italian during the summer of
1973, I spent a good deal of time wondering and praying about this
question posed to me by others: In what way are others essential
to my relationship with God? In what way are they indispensably
present? Other people are obviously crucially important and integral, irreplaceable. I spend most of my life with them and (hope-
fully) much of it for them. They enclose relationships of friendship,
love, and wisdom that make up much of the richness of life. This
seems obvious. But how are they absolutely essential and indispensable to my hope for a relationship with God—so much so that
if they were not present, I would have no relationship with God at
all? That is what I mean by "absolutely essential."

These puzzling, confused reflections were triggered by a foundational statement of Cardinal Newman, taken with its full force: that there are simply "two and two only absolute and luminously self-evident beings, myself and my Creator."[1] But are others essential, that is, an absolutely necessary part of my conscious life with God, my affectivity, and my actions—so much so that if they were not somehow or other consciously present I would have no relationship with God, or for that matter, with myself? This formed the context in which I hear and understand something of the question that Jesus asks of Mary at Cana: "What is [this] to me and to you?"[2] It asks how we include essentially within our lives those we might otherwise forget as we go about the business of our lives.

The dialectical form of the question, of course, realizes a Semitic idiom. It asks: Do we have something in common between us here?[3] It probes: What business is that of ours? Or perhaps: How does that involve *me*—and not just you? Or, as in this question: How are *we* involved? This interrogation calls into question whether there is any common concern here or even a common passion in which we are united, in which we come together into a "we." What is here to unite us in a common concern, a single identity in a care that we share? Why are we involved? How is this a concern of me and you?

Jesus's question looks like a refusal, but that is deceptive. It is easily noted that no request has been made. Mary simply comments, the way anyone might, that the wine is gone. There is no directive, no command. No request is made of her son. The mother appropriates

1. John Henry Newman, *Apologia Pro Vita Sua*, ed. Martin J. Svaglic (Oxford: Clarendon, 1967), 17–18: "I retained it [the feeling of this inward conversion] till the age of twenty-one, when it gradually faded away; but I believe that it had some influence on my opinions, in the direction of those childish imaginations which I have already mentioned, viz. in isolating me from the objects which surrounded me, in confirming me in my mistrust of the reality of material phenomena, and making me rest in the thought of two and two only absolute and luminously self-evident beings, myself and my Creator."

2. Raymond Brown, SS, *The Gospel according to John: I–XII*, Anchor Bible (Garden City, NY: Doubleday, 1966), 99.

3. Brown, *The Gospel according to John: I–XII*, 90.

the shattering embarrassment, the pain of others, and represents it to Jesus. But he reads much more than that into her comment. Jesus transforms her remark and takes it as if it were a request. He then meets a request that has not been made with what seems to be its refusal. He refers to Mary, his mother, as "woman"—the way "woman" would appear in John 19 before the cross, and in the sign that appears in the heavens in Revelation 12. "Woman" transposes the symbolic significance of this interchange into what it is to become for all times and all places. Mary becomes the symbol of the entire church.

Mary ignores the refusal that seems to have been made of a request that had not been put, and carries this interchange one depth deeper, ignoring the surface meaning of what Jesus has just said. In Rudolf Bultmann's words: "The mother has understood her son: all she can do now is to await the miracle worker. So she directs the servants to do whatever Jesus tells them."[4]

Contrast the subtlety of the progressive understanding of the Lukan Mary that pondered the nativity events in her heart with the continual obtuseness of the disciples, especially after the question to Philip. Mary comments—and Jesus understands what is beneath. Jesus questions Mary—and she discerns the actual depth and meaning informing the seeming denial. She understands that this concern touches him so much that she can direct the servers to a more general openness and availability: "Do whatever he commands you." Why did she have to say that? Would the narrative not have found them obeying Jesus without this directive? The Gospel discloses that the servants did what they did at the direction of Mary. This seems to be strongly paradigmatic of her continual influence within the church.

In fact, are there not times in the history of the church in which the influence of Mary has made the influence of Jesus both present and directive in a way it otherwise would not have been? In the Gua-

---

4. Rudolf Bultmann, *The Gospel of John: A Commentary,* trans. G. R. Beasley-Murray, R. W. N. Hoare, and J. K. Riches (Philadelphia: Westminster, 1971), 117.

dalupe culture of Mexico? In the piety of nineteenth-century France? In the ordinary piety and understanding of Catholics for centuries when the liturgy was in Latin, translations forbidden, the Eucharist at a great distance and seldom received, and much of the clergy lost in class isolation? Is it not simply a palpable fact that the presence of Mary and the historic identification of Mary with the poor and the unlettered gave them a unique and powerful access to Jesus, and that her symbolic, unrealized presence and influence within the church kept them Catholic in a deeper sense than may have met a theologian's eye? Here is the mystery and source of authentic Marian piety: Mary giving birth to Jesus, her endless service to the church.

For this question of Jesus continues through history to stand before his mother, and in her, to stand before the church: "How are we involved in the needs of these people?" It is of great importance to the life and mission of the church that we hear this question. For it has been and is shockingly easy not to see human social misery or to take it for granted as part of the intractable social situation. Examples abound even in the lives of men and women great in sophisticated theological knowledge and heroic in sanctity.

The only time, as I recall, that the factories of Birmingham in the nineteenth century—where women and small children were working twelve hours a day in wretched conditions—figured in the diaries and writings of John Henry Cardinal Newman was in the record he made of his visit to one of them very late in his life. His visit was meant to ensure that the Catholic women would be allowed to attend Mass and that the Christian instruction for Catholics would be within the creed. Amid the terrible poverty that suffused Birmingham, he makes note of nothing else.

And what of the great Baron von Hügel—one of the supreme masters of spiritual theology in the twentieth century? One of his friends who "lodged with him for some years 'recalled the squalor in which the baron's servants lived.'"[5]

---

5. James J. Kelly, *Baron Friedrich von Hügel's Philosophy of Religion* (Leuven: Leuven University Press, 1983), 211.

Newman was not indifferent to the poor; indeed, he worked among them for years. Nor did Baron von Hügel consciously exploit his help. They simply did not see this kind of social need and class poverty for what it was. Social structures and widespread poverty with its sufferings were simply taken for granted. This kind of social myopia threatens all human beings. Even the greatest men and women have profound class limitations. This demonstrates the serious and continual need for the question of Jesus to Mary. It calls all human beings into painful judgment. The church, the local Christian community, its theologians—the question of Jesus calls them also into judgment. In every aspect of life, one can hear the searing question to Mary: "What is this to me and to you?"

Christians have heard this text so many times and in so many ways that it can be dulled by its repetition if it is not searchingly applied. This Gospel is to be insistently proclaimed year after year within the church, so that Christians might come to see what they do not adequately see and feel, so that the question would touch, even shape, their understanding of what God through his Spirit is calling them to. The church is summoned by God never to forget, in its array of talents, promises, and temporal successes, the suffering of the marginalized. The question to Mary is essential to this call. The question, in its own haunting way, surmounts the banality of repetition and offers to those who can hear it the meaning of Christian life. That can be the reason why the social doctrine of the church can be far more radical than that of either American political party.

Seeing the Suffering

Leaders and religious in and outside the church can be so isolated that they become incapable of hearing this call in any demanding way, in a way that would cause a revolution in their own appropriation of reality. Isolated from such insecurity and pain, a priest can easily find himself unconsciously alienated from the lived experience, the searching anxieties, and the poignant needs of the very poor. A closed clerical subculture can develop, and has developed, within the church. A priest can see the migrant workers bent over in the fields in California as he drives by on the highway. The priest can see it—he can even reflect on it—but it may not impinge upon his life or tear at his sensibilities; it may not form the stuff of his examination of conscience, of what he spontaneously represents before God. He can become more a spectator than a participant in these lives, in their misery. He neither suffers their lot nor experiences their need. He may only regret it. And this distance is destroying the church.

This is to talk about lived experience—not privations calculated at a distance. Instead of having a common ground, a common concern that unites Christians with Christ in the very poor, they can move in isolation from it and in some emotional indifference. "They simply don't get it." If, unlike Mary, they do not appropriate with some depth of experience and passion the needs of others, they become less and less those who can even hear the question contained within the human situation addressed to them, less and less those who can turn to the Lord with any experienced poignancy and say: "They have no wine." The statement has become insistently a question about life itself.

One has only to raise one's eyes to see this poverty and suffering.

Those parents who watch their children grow up without education, without much hope for a better life; the migrants who shift with the crops in the Southwest, knowing bitterly that their children are condemned to repeat the lives of their parents—"They have no wine."

The millions of old, hidden away in our cities or in dreadful convalescent hospitals, who with very little must eke out lives of threat, worry, and terror on minimal subsistence—"They have no wine."

The despised or feared or uneducated—men and women, especially the poor in the inner city, the impoverished Spanish speakers, Native Americans, and African Americans, whose lives are terrorized by the violence on their streets and the hopelessness of ever getting enough education or capital to escape—"They have no wine."

The debtor nations, attempting to pay off their debts by progressively and unconscionably lowering the living standards of the poor—"They have no wine."

Women demeaned and threatened in almost every city in the United States, by violence and their disproportionate level of financial insecurity, patronized and discriminated against at the highest level of decision making even within the church, and by their level of poverty in the world—"They have no wine."

In all this misery, the question of Jesus returns Christians back to themselves: "What is this to me and to you?" What is this world of endless sorrow to us? How should it shape our lives?

Christians become more Christian as they realize in themselves the mysterious promise that is the church—and what it means to become church. The church, in its turn, becomes more itself the more it realizes the call of the mother of God in her appropriation of the pain and sorrow of others. This may be the embarrassment of a wedding couple, or the pain of her son at his death, or the hidden church praying for the Spirit that would give it insight and courage. The church becomes more the church as the pain of the human race comes more and more into its consciousness and into its effective action, its experience and understanding and affectivity—as the condition of human beings gets a stronger purchase on the lives of Christians.

Responding in Love

The effect of this ignorance and indifference has been the destruction of much of the church as an effective agent within the world.

For others are absolutely essential to one's union with God.

Without this love, there would be no Christian relationship to God. Here is where one becomes capable of responding to the question of Jesus: "What is this to me and to you?" Wisely Thomas Aquinas insisted that the love of charity in which we love God is the same capacity of charity by which we love other human beings. It is in charity that one becomes capable of responding fully to the question of Jesus. Here is one of the great lessons that contemporary religious can learn from the questions of Jesus.

In 1944, when Roger Schutz wanted to form his ecumenical monastic community, he determined with Max Thurian to locate it in one of the most de-Christianized sections of France. And so he chose Taizé in Burgundy, in the neighborhood of what had for centuries been the greatest and most extensive monastery in Europe, the Abbey of Cluny. It is not strange, although it is paradoxical, that this was the neighborhood that he lighted upon. For the most de-Christianized places in France are the sites of what were once the wealthiest and most powerful monasteries in France.

One afternoon, at a reception for Cardinal Daniels, the former primate of Belgium, I mentioned this curious fact to him. His response: "Of course, you will find exactly the same situation in Belgium." If one looks over the social and religious history of Italy, one will find that the most extensively communist areas are in what had been the Papal States.

Why is this the case, all Catholics must ask themselves—why so often was the legacy of centuries of establishment, of institutional productivity and security and great religious art, frequently a profound alienation and de-Christianization? Why is there a cultural absence of God where those very institutions that should have ministered to his presence were so powerful? And to be more concrete and particular, does one find anything similar in the United States—a powerful presence but a growing disbelief, alienation, disgust, and distance? Part of the reason may well be that very power and wealth. Perhaps because local churches and large Christian communities that possessed, for whatever reasons, political power and extensive holdings became strangers to the massive social inequity and outrageous poverty and humiliation of so many, and came to accept comfortably a social structure that was impoverishing and unjust. Did they inevitably come to trust in the status quo, no matter how unjust, to feel secure in the presence of what they had, and to fall under the terrible condemnation of the prophet?

> Cursed is the man who trust in man
> > and makes flesh his arm,
> > whose heart turns away from the LORD.
> He is like a shrub in the desert,
> > and shall not see any good come.
> He shall dwell in the parched places of the wilderness,
> > in an uninhabited salt land. (Jer. 17:5–6)

Among the many stories of Saint Francis of Assisi, one in particular bears on this lesson. The story goes that Francis was being shown the Lateran palace by Pope Innocent III, and the vision was one of splendor. The pope is reported to have said, "It is the same Church, but we can no longer say with the apostle Peter: 'Gold and silver I have not.'" To which Francis answered, "Nor do you have the power to say, 'In the name of Jesus of Nazareth, walk'" (see Acts 3:1–7).

⫸ 8 ⫷

"HOW ARE WE TO BUY BREAD,
SO THAT THESE PEOPLE MAY EAT?"

Lifting up his eyes, then, and seeing that a multitude was coming to him, Jesus said to Philip, "How are we to buy bread, so that these people may eat?" (John 6:5)

Making Room for the Impossible

This question of Jesus is much more than a simple question. It is more than an attempt to bring Philip to reflect upon his immediate capabilities and experience. Experience could never handle what was before and all around Jesus: the massive crowd, the lateness of the hour, the press upon them, the dogged weariness from the work of early ministry. The Gospel says explicitly that Jesus was "testing" Philip. Perhaps even tempting him. The overwhelming temptation was to look at what had to be done, to understand despondently that it was simply absurd to demand such a performance, ludicrously beyond human resources. Neither Philip's imaginary money nor Andrew's two fish and five loaves are enough. They are obviously not enough. Philip turns to Jesus only to itemize his patent powerlessness. The battle should never have been engaged. A sinking frustration surrounds the very question that will emerge: the realization that Philip is in every way inadequate to fulfill this mad demand.

This pericope is not the place to thrash around the value of 200 denarii or to weigh out five loaves and two fish. Further, one must attend to the particular day on which this question arises. It is the Passover, the feast of the Jews. This is the transforming intervention of God into the hopelessness of an enslaved people. It bespeaks the power of God in utter weakness. The question of Jesus draws Philip to the power and intervention of God. But this is precisely what Philip does not grasp—though he blindly and paradoxically is following the guidance of Jesus. Rudolf Schnackenburg correctly notes that "Philip does not hear the appeal to his faith concealed in Jesus' question. He is without understanding in the face of Jesus' claim."[1] An impossible demand informs the question addressed to Philip by Jesus. Is all hope gone, Philip, so that Jesus's call and your limits launch you into the ridiculously abstract? Is there any place for the impossible, for making any sense of this question of Jesus? This is a typical challenge for those who would give themselves in any way to serve the mystery of Jesus.

Trusting God

This is so typical, so paradigmatic of God's mysterious dealing with human beings who find themselves caught up in the claim of the divine. Over and over again, God forces human beings, especially those who are close to him, into a crisis of profound inadequacy. There is the felt destruction of any support system: "When I add up my accomplishments and talents, when I attempt to recall my religious experience, and even my sins and repentance, my intentions and convictions, the history of my prayer, all of these seem

---

1. Rudolf Schnackenburg, *The Gospel according to John,* vol. 2, *Commentary on Chapters 5–12* (New York: Seabury, 1980), 15.

trite and empty—nothing is adequate." Time after time God will bring those who would follow Christ into a situation in which they are starkly faced in so many different ways with the simple but concrete question: Do you trust me with your life? This experience of the absurd demands of Jesus brings, even forces, the question.

To be questioned in this way has its own evolution. One must first experience radical inadequacy—the profound human poverty of the moment—like the poor person of the Sermon on the Mount. Having nothing, he is blessed if he looks only to God for the direction, the support, and the definition of his life. The invisible God becomes rock. And this becomes his question: Do I finally trust you even within my glaring inadequacies, with my lack of resources, even when there is not even the experience of trusting you, but only the shaking emotions of fear, confusion, and uncertainty? So much of the buoyant feelings of American self-consciousness and self-assuredness dissolves before this challenge.

Bearing Witness to the Power of God

There is a tendency among us Americans, common and obvious enough, recommended by common sense and successful practice, to evaluate a person's aptitude for a life task or a profession or a career by listing the person's strengths. Elizabeth speaks well, possesses an able mind, exhibits superior talents for leadership and debate—she would make a good lawyer. John has fine judgment, a scientific bent of mind, obvious manual dexterity, and deep human concerns—he would make a splendid surgeon.[2]

Now, the tendency is to transfer this method of positive evaluation to the promises of any religious attraction as well, to mea-

2. These reflections by the author in this section and the next first appeared as "Because Beset with Weakness . . . ," in *To Be a Priest: Perspectives on Vocation and Ordination*, ed. Robert E. Terwilliger and Urban T. Holmes (New York: Seabury, 1975), 125–30.

sure a person by the person's gifts and talents, to line up a history of previous positive achievements and the capacity for more, to understand the promise for the future in terms of the accomplishments of the past, and to make the religious call within his or her life contingent upon the attainments of personality or grace. Because a man is religiously serious, prayerful, socially adept, and intellectually perceptive, and possesses interior integrity, sound common sense, and habits of hard work, he would make a fine priest or minister.

This simple transfer can be disastrously misguided. Such an evaluative procedure is obviously reasonable, even necessary, but it can be profoundly deceptive and misleading. For how many years has it led to misinterpretation and misguidance? It is certainly reasonable that a person should calculate personal resources before building a tower or engaging in battle. The Scriptures even recommend this kind of calculation (Luke 14:28). It is necessary that one look to the direction God is giving human lives also through their experienced desires and natural orientations and capacities. All this is true, but it can be meretricious. This transfer invites serious error if the positive inventory is taken as comprehensively adequate. For there is a different question, one proper to any form of Christian ministry: Is this person weak enough to be a servant of the gospel of Christ?

For the mystery of God and of anything that is caught up in the divine is incomprehensibly beyond the powers of men and women. Their lives have to bear witness, not only to their developed capacities and humane qualities, but even more importantly to the power of God drawing and working in them (cf. 2 Cor. 12:8–10). This life with its call and its selection, and its mysterious consecrations, profoundly particularizes itself around the cross and must be specified by the cross, especially in times of serious personal crisis and a pervasive sense of weakness and inadequacy.

There are times, and there must be times, essential to any religious consecration or ministerial dedication, when talents and spontaneous interests fail, when there is only the sterile and confused experience of this failure; when personality and friends are inadequate for any meaning and value and seem very distant; when the sustaining presence of God evanesces and one has to struggle to believe that G-O-D is more than simply three letters; when theology and religious language seem unreal or futile, sterile, and abstract; when the men and women one has counted on and deeply admired have walked away; when temptation and weakness and pain are so much more a part of the felt experience and one becomes weary with the impossibility of the task. "How are we to buy bread, so that these people may eat?"

John of the Cross classically called such moments the "dark night of the soul," while Ignatius of Loyola expected such desolation to occur during the making of the *Spiritual Exercises*, and provided for it. This liability for interior suffering can and does occur at any time during a person's movement toward God, or better, during God's movement upon the person. Broader and more extensive, it occurs not just in the moments that possess recognizable names, but throughout the lives of men and women who have given their lives to God, when pain and desolation seem everywhere.

There are times that demand a fidelity or a compassion that seems overwhelmingly beyond one's power, and one looks around or within—and finds that the resources are simply not there: one is not clever enough, or secure enough or educated enough, or holy enough to meet the needs that cry out and must be met.

Being Weak Enough for Service

Here the question of Jesus comes to the priest or the religious or the engaged and apostolic Christian: "How are we to buy bread, so that these people may eat?" It is the question of desperation. Philip understood the task. He also understood the impossibility of the task, and saw that it was utterly beyond his powers. It is here, in the challenge and the commission of this moment, that the religious person is most liable to suffering.[3] For it is here that the person experiences both the wants of others and his or her own inescapable poverty. And so the question becomes "Can one live with this experience of profound weakness—weakness as the liability to suffering—since this weakness is inescapable in one's vocation?" Thus there necessarily emerges another question about any Christian vocation: "Is this person weak enough to be a priest, so liable to suffering that he will not depend upon himself, but rather live dependent upon the hidden, sustaining power of God— depending upon the power of God, not upon his experience of the power of God?" In this understanding, the criteria for judging an authentic Christian vocation change immeasurably.

Is this person deficient enough not to be able to ward off significant suffering from his or her life, so that the person can live with a certain amount of failure and can feel what it is to be an average person? Is there any history of confusion, of self-doubt, of interior anguish? Has the individual had to deal with fear, come to terms with frustrations, or accept profoundly deflated expectations? These are critical questions, and they probe for weakness. Why weakness? Why this liability to pain and suffering? Because, according to the letter to the Hebrews, it is precisely in this deficiency, in this particular liability to suffering, that the efficacy of the ministry and priesthood of Christ is found. "For because he himself has suffered and been tempted, he is able to help those who are tempted. . . . For we have not a high priest who is unable to sympathize with our weaknesses, but one who in every respect has been tempted as we are, yet without sinning. . . . He can deal

---

3. It is very important to emphasize that what is said here about the vocation to the priesthood is true of any form of serious religious consecration to ministry, such as religious life and apostolic commitments. It is grammatically awkward to move between the various forms of religious consecration, but it is imperative to note the claim that the religious person makes on all of them.

gently with the ignorant and wayward, since he himself is beset with weakness" (Heb. 2:18; 4:15; 5:2).

"Beset with weakness"? How critically important it is to take very seriously the conjunction between any Christian ministry and weakness; how important, that one dwells upon this sense of deficiency even as an essential part of this vocation! Otherwise, one can secularize these lives into an amalgam of desires and talents, and one can feel that any pervasive liability and weakness is a threat to apostolic consecration; that it indicates that one should rethink what was previously resolved; that it is symptomatic of one never genuinely called, that one does not have the resources to complete what one once thought was free destiny and which once spoke to generosity and fidelity.

What is meant by weakness? Not the experience of sin. Indeed, almost its opposite. Weakness is the experience of a peculiar liability for suffering; a profound sense of inability both to do and to protect; an inability, even after great effort, to author or to perform as we should want, to effect what we had determined; an inability to succeed with the completeness that we might have hoped for. Weakness is the openness to the humiliations and sufferings that issue in the inability to secure one's own future, to protect ourselves from any adversity, to live with easy clarity and assurance, or to ward off shame, pain, and even interior anguish.

If human beings are clever enough or devious enough or poised enough, they can limit horizons and expectations and accomplish pretty much what they would want. They can secure their perimeters and live without an acknowledged sense of failure or inadequacy or shame before their temperaments or their tasks. For in each of these, they experience weakness at the heart of their lives. But it does not give the lie to their vocations. Rather, paradoxically, this weakness can confirm or validate their vocations. For this experience, rather than militating against ministry, is part of its essential structure. The liability for suffering forms a critically important indication of the call of God, that terrible sinking sense of incapacity when Moses was presented his mission and Jeremiah his vocation, that profound conviction of sinfulness when the vision of God rose before Isaiah and demanded response.

There is a classic comparison running in different directions through Western philosophy between Socrates and Christ, a judgment between them in human excellence. Socrates went to his death with calmness and poise. He accepted the judgment of the court, discoursed on the alternatives suggested by death and on the dialectical indications of immortality, found no cause for fear, drank the poison, and died. Jesus was almost hysterical with terror and fear, offering "loud cries and tears, to him who was able to save him from death" (Heb. 5:7; cf. John 12:27). He looked repeatedly to his friends for comfort and prayed for an escape from death, and he found neither. Finally he established control over himself and moved into his death in prayerful silence and lonely isolation, even into the terrible interior suffering of the hidden divinity, the dark absence of God.

I once thought that the difference was because Socrates and Jesus suffered different deaths, the one so much more terrible than the other, the pain and agony of the cross so overshadowing the release of the hemlock. But now I think that this explanation, though correct as far as it goes, is superficial and secondary.

I believe now that Jesus was a more profoundly weak man than Socrates, that is, more liable to suffering, to physical pain, and to disheartening weariness; more sensitive to human rejection and contempt; more affected by love and hate. Socrates never wept over Athens. Socrates never expressed sorrow and pain over the betrayal of friends. He was self-possessed and integral, never over-extended, convinced that the just man could never suffer genuine hurt. And for this reason, Socrates—one of the greatest, most heroic persons ever to exist, a paradigm of what humanity can achieve within the individual—was a philosopher. And for the same reason, Jesus of Nazareth was a priest—ambiguous, suffering, mysterious, and salvific.

The priest or anyone engaged in the compassion of Christian ministry must also be liable to suffering. He must become like what he touches—the body of Christ. Obviously, the ordinary person understands the priest or Christian minister primarily and imaginatively through the Eucharist within the church. But what is the Eucharist? The body of Christ? Yes, certainly, but how understood? How does Christ conceive and present this, his body? The question is an important one. Psychologists maintain that people understand themselves in terms of their spontaneous body images, that what they sense and feel about their bodies is what they sense and feel about themselves, that as they perceive their bodies so they perceive themselves.

How in the Scriptures and in the liturgy does Jesus perceive his body? It is a body that is broken for us; a blood that is shed for us (Luke 22:17–20). Jesus understands himself as a sacrificed self, that is, effective only by passing through his destruction into an eternal, resurrected life, giving the Spirit in life and freedom to human beings only because he himself has moved through death and terror and achieved new life. The liturgy celebrates "the great mystery that he has left us." The Eucharist only achieves its graced entrance into our lives in communion, that is, if broken and distributed. It is the liability of Christ to undergo this breaking and distributing, his ability to be symbolically broken and shed, that makes the life of the apostolic Christian effective and Eucharist possible. How paradoxical this mystery is! The strength and the efficacy of the priesthood of Christ and all Christian ministry lie precisely in the weakness that seems to threaten them. The sensitivity and openness to discouragement and suffering and death contribute then to the mystery of the priesthood of Christ, however it is shared. Now why?

Weakness and the suffering it entails relate human beings profoundly to one another. Weakness allows them to feel and to share with others the human condition, the struggle and darkness and anguish that call out for salvation. To be a developed human being, one necessarily accepts a certain amount of suffering into one's life without bitterness. It is hard to get at this acceptance, since so much in Western civilization attempts to disguise it or affects to despise it. One of the most debilitating aspects of American society is that it does not authentically admit the cost in a struggle and almost never allows anguish or real fear to surface. Yet most of us must struggle to make a living, must wonder about our future and about our sense of personal value in a market-value-driven economy, must deal with the half-articulated and half-understood problems of our children, must fear what our death will be like—what it will mean to die. We must deal with the temptations to believe that life is without meaning, that actions in themselves are inconsequential and selfish, and that other people are to be used.

Being a priest or minister of the gospel does not mean—must not mean—that the Christian is excised from all of that struggle, as if called to deal with temptations from a higher eminence; it does not mean that the meaning and value and fidelity to the gospel have been completed in our lives, and that we now deal out of our strength with the lives of others. But God has called the Christian to the salvation of all human beings, and there is no salvation without incarnation.

The mystery of salvation encompasses all human beings, as Christ is a human being, and human beings can understand and respond to the degree that they feel themselves "beset with weakness" (Heb. 5:2). This is to share in the ministry of Christ. If part of human life becomes a subtle, only occasionally noticed effort to maintain a daily sense of call in a culture that increasingly finds it anachronistic and dying—a struggle against a sense of barrenness when God seems so distant, so unreal, and yet his reality is the one thing to which we have given our entire lives; an exertion to deal sensitively and honestly with nagging preoccupations, with difficult colleagues, with distant superiors in a context that seems lifeless and without promise—then it is indispensably important to remember that those who serve the gospel are called to be human beings, called to enter as Christ so deeply into human suffering—the human condition. Temptations and desolations become the grace of God calling to fidelity and to a more profound sensitivity those who are similarly embattled. This realizes in the Gospels themselves the ancient wisdom of Aeschylus: "A human being must suffer to become wise."[4] Secondly, weakness more profoundly relates us to God, because it provides the ambit or the arena in which his grace can be disclosed, his sustaining presence can reveal itself, and his power can become manifest. This is why this weakness contradicts expectations and stands as almost the contrary of sin. Weakness is the context for the epiphany of the Lord; it is the night in which he appears—not always as felt reassurance, but more often as a hidden power to continue, faithful even when one does not feel the strength, even when fidelity means simply putting one foot in front of the other.

Paul saw his own life's history in this litany of reversals or sufferings, as linking moments of weakness, but transformed through the supporting power of Christ: "I will all the more gladly boast of my weaknesses, that the power of Christ may rest upon me. For the sake of Christ, then, I am content with weaknesses, insults, hardships, persecutions, and calamities; for when I am weak, then I am strong" (2 Cor. 12:9–10).

Ministry in Weakness

In these moments, those given to Christian ministry often discover what their vocation means, as the power of God is disclosed in the continuity of their lives, a fidelity that weakness would only seem to undermine but actually supports as it evokes the presence of the Lord. Weakness enters into the vocation of the Lord, our call

4. Aeschylus, *The Agamemnon*, trans. Louis MacNeice (New York: Harcourt, Brace and Co., 1937), 19.

upon him. It is this night, and the heavy work of rowing against the storm and threatening waves, that brings him to us. It is not that the life of the Christian in some form of ministry would ideally have been a more comfortable reality—without struggle, self-doubt, or suffering—but that circumstances have unfortunately introduced obduracy and humiliations and a sense of incapacity. Quite the contrary. It is in and through this night that a Christian is joined to Christ; as it is in and through this night that the Christian learns that he or she can trust the Lord—can call out to Jesus in faith, even when this seems the most lifeless thing to do—and finds that Jesus Christ is enough. After a massive stroke that left him debilitated, Pedro Arrupe offered this to his Jesuit brothers gathered at the thirty-third General Congregation: "More than ever I find myself in the hands of God. This is what I have wanted all my life from my youth. But now there is a difference; the initiative is entirely with God. It is indeed a profound spiritual experience to know and feel myself so totally in God's hands."[5]

Only in this way will what has been taught and preached and urged upon others become part of Christian life. So here we learn, as in no other place, the commitment of our lives in trust to the Lord. It is in this experience, the experience of personal weakness and of having read even limitations as the presence of Christ, of having trusted in him in darkness, and having found in this way that one can actually trust him—it is this experience that joins Christ to his disciples, as he comes to them walking on the waters.

There is a collective consequence that follows from all of this. Christian communities must make such a life possible for one another. For it is not just the individual who must be weak enough to participate in the weakness of Christ, but also the community itself. They must support one another in weakness, forgiving one

---

5. Jim Campbell, "Pedro Arrupe, S.J.," Ignatian Spirituality, accessed August, 13, 2014; http://www.ignatianspirituality.com/ignatian-voices/20th-century-ignatian-voices/pedro-arrupe-sj/.

another's daily faults and carrying one another's burdens. It would be absurd to maintain that weakness is an essential part of the Christian vocation, a participation in the priesthood of Christ, and then to belittle those who are deficient; to resent those who are insensitive, unsophisticated, or clumsy; to allow disagreements to become hostilities. It would be a dreadful thing to reject, under one criterion or another, those whom God has called and consecrated to himself.

The sad fact stands, however, that it is frequently no great trick to get religious men or women to turn on one another in some form of condemnation. Wars, even personal wars, are terrible realities, and the most horrible of these are often self-righteously religious. For deceived or split off under the guise of the good, under the rubrics of orthodoxy or liberality, of community or of personal freedom, even of holiness itself, factions of religious men and women can slowly disintegrate into pettiness or cynicism or hostility or bitterness, so that "the last state of that man becomes worse than the first" (Luke 11:26). In this way the Christian church becomes divided.

Christian ministers are of the same stuff as other human beings, and they also depend upon men and women to mediate the unconditioned love of God to their weakness. The command of Christ, that we should love one another as he has loved us, is more than a general norm of total benevolence; it is a particular mission: he cared—out of his own weakness—for our weakness, and so became our Eucharist.

ᴡ(9)ᴍ

"DO YOU NOT BELIEVE THAT I AM
IN THE FATHER AND THE FATHER IN ME?"

Philip said to him, "Lord, show us the Fa-
ther, and we shall be satisfied." Jesus said
to him, "Have I been with you so long, and
yet you do not know me, Philip? He who has
seen me has seen the Father; how can you say,
'Show us the Father'? Do you not believe that
I am in the Father and the Father in me?"
(John 14:8–10)

The "Place" Where We Find God

This may seem the most abstruse of all the questions the Gospel
narratives have placed before Jesus's disciples. In an earlier section
of this Gospel (10:38), Jesus had stated this mysterious "formula of
reciprocal immanence," that he is in the Father and the Father is in
him. This assertion would for centuries serve as critical matter for
dogmatic theology or apologetics, but it does not appear so easily
and so readily to be the content of prayer, that is, for the interpersonal relationship of human beings with God that one could call
"a knowledge of God." But in many ways, this mysterious location
of Jesus within the Father and the Father's place within Jesus may

actually, for a religious person or any religious community, pose the sharpest, the most profound directives to guide and identify the human unity with God. Thus one should underline that in this question, as the medieval Cistercian William of St. Thierry has insisted, one is brought to Christ, as the "place" of God, where above all God can be found by human beings and human beings can be found by God. In this age of rising atheism and religious skepticism, the prayer of William of St. Thierry becomes even more pertinent:

> O Truth, answer, I implore you! "Master, where do you dwell?"
> "Come," he said, "and see." "Do you not believe that I am in the Father, and the Father is in me?" Thanks be to you, O Lord! We have achieved something after all! We have found your "place"! For your "place" is your Father, and you are the Father's "place"! In this place, you are localized. But this localization of yours, this limiting in space, is far more lofty and mysterious than any absence of place. This localization is the unity of the Father and the Son. . . . [Now] do all you can, my soul, not so much by the exercise of reason as by activity of love.[1]

Jesus is above all the "place" where one is to find God.

The Death of God

If someone wanted to identify a single figure that prophetically ushered in the religious repudiations of the contemporary West, one could not do better than say the name Friedrich Nietzsche. It was Nietzsche who formed the story of the madman, the one who lit a lamp in the bright morning and ran into the marketplace,

---

1. William of St. Thierry, "On Contemplating God: Prayer, Meditations," in *The Works of William of St. Thierry*, vol. 1, trans. Sister Penelope, CSMV, Cistercian Fathers 3 (Spencer, MA: Cistercian Publications, 1971), 73.

and cried out incessantly: "I seek God! I seek God." As Nietzsche's parable unfolds, the madman screams: "We have killed him—you and I. All of us are his murderers. But how could we do this? How could we wipe away the entire horizon? What were we doing when we unchained this earth from its sun?" The episode reaches its end as the madman wanders into several churches, and there in the empty sanctuaries strikes up his *requiem aeternam deo*.[2] Nietzsche's requiem in the sanctuaries of Europe will announce for the centuries the death of God.

But what does this death mean in Nietzsche? It does not mean in any simpleminded way that God had been once alive, an actual being, but now had in some way perished, that he had abandoned the earth or dialectically passed into something other, as so many of the death-of-God theologians in the late twentieth century proposed. Nietzsche's myth lies a million miles away from that proposal. For the death of God in Nietzsche is not an ontological statement but an epistemological statement, an understanding of culture. At the very beginning of the fifth book of *Die fröhliche Wissenschaft*, Nietzsche spells out precisely the meaning of this parable: "The greatest recent event—that 'God is dead,' that the belief in the Christian God has become unbelievable—is already beginning to cast its first shadows over Europe."[3] Belief itself is no longer credible. Faith in God was gradually becoming an impossibility, even a dated absurdity.

Contemporaneous with Nietzsche, the great John Henry Newman, in England, saw the same shadows lengthen over what had once been Christian Europe.

> I look out of myself into the world of men, and there I see a sight which fills me with unspeakable distress. The world seems simply to give the lie to that great truth of which my whole being

2. Friedrich Nietzsche, *The Gay Science*, ed. Bernard Williams, trans. Josefine Nauckhoff and Adrian Del Caro (New York: Cambridge University Press, 2001), 119–21.

3. Nietzsche, *The Gay Science*, 199.

is so full [the existence of God]. . . . In these latter days, in like manner, outside the Catholic Church things are tending—with far greater rapidity than in that old time from the circumstance of the age,—to atheism in one shape or other. What a scene, what a prospect, does the whole of Europe present at this day! and not only Europe, but every government and every civilization through the world, which is under the influence of the European mind.[4]

Nietzsche and Newman spoke of tendencies, movements, great drifts of culture that took their rise in modernity. In the contemporary centuries, these prophecies have reached massive fulfillment. One can encounter this omnipresent void in the pervasive inability to believe or even to care, or in the profound reaches of such disappointment and sorrows as one sees in the figure of Dr. Delbende in Georges Bernanos's *Diary of a Country Priest*:

At fourteen, Dr. Delbende had intended to be a missionary; he lost his faith in the course of medical studies. He was the favorite student of a certain very famous doctor—I forget his name—and all his friends prophesied a brilliant future for him. Everyone was amazed when he started a practice in this out-of-the-way place. At that time he said he hadn't the money to take his final degrees and in any case, he was in a bad state of health, due to overwork. But he was inconsolable at not being able to believe. He had some extraordinary ways. He would hurl questions at a crucifix hanging on his bedroom wall. Sometimes he would sob at its feet with his head in his hands, or he would even defy it, shaking his fist.[5]

---

4. John Henry Newman, *Apologia Pro Vita Sua,* ed. Martin J. Svaglic (Oxford: Clarendon, 1967), 216–19.

5. Georges Bernanos, *The Diary of a Country Priest* (New York: Carroll and Graf, 2002), 116.

"Not being able to believe." For so many contemporaries, this raw desire for eternal meaning, such as it is, gives way eventually to a working despair; indeed, this longing, in its contradiction, simply increases the despair. Philip in the Gospel narrative gives utterance to what has been for so many centuries the defeated longings of the ages—"Show us the Father, and we will be satisfied." But even in Freud, the haunting presence of unrequited sorrow often takes its resignations with a dismissive cynicism: "We should tell ourselves that it would be very nice if there were a God that created the world and was a benevolent Providence, and if there were a moral order in the universe and an afterlife; but it is a very striking fact that all this is exactly as we are bound to wish it to be. And it would be more remarkable still if our wretched, ignorant and downtrodden ancestors had succeeded in solving all of these difficult riddles of the universe."[6]

Freud's ideal of religious fulfillment often comes across as little more than an attempt to untangle a puzzle, to solve the riddle of the universe. Interpersonal longing and love play no part in it.

Similarly, of all the groups in the United States, those most alienated from any religious beliefs seem to be the intellectuals and the professional elites in journalism and media. In *Dreams of a Final Theory*, Steven Weinberg observes: "Among today's scientists, I am probably somewhat atypical in caring about such things. On the rare occasions when conversations over lunch or tea touch on matters of religion, the strongest reaction expressed by most of my fellow physicists is a mild surprise and amusement that anyone still takes all of that seriously."[7]

But it is not intellectuals only who embody this spirit. Atheism or disbelief runs like a river through much of ordinary consciousness. In *The Heart Is a Lonely Hunter*, Mick says, "I don't believe in

6. Sigmund Freud, *The Future of an Illusion* (New York: Norton, 1961), 42.
7. Steven Weinberg, *Dreams of a Final Theory: The Scientist's Search for the Ultimate Laws of Nature* (New York: Pantheon, 1992), 256.

God any more than I do Santa Claus."[8] But many centuries before, Bossuet had already registered something of this for all human beings: "There is an atheism concealed in all hearts, which is diffused in all our actions; God counts for nothing."[9]

Do contemporary Christians not also hear these voices? Are they not an ineluctable part of their prayer—the social context of the commitments and of the company of their lives? Further, do they say nothing about the precisely Christian character and even urgency of the call upon a Christian presence today? Does their religious anguish or despair not give some shape to what the Christian must be about?

Finding Christ in a Community Called Church

What Philip is asking of Jesus carries not only the desire or the despairs of Everyman, but also their implicit conditions, the anger and the protest that one is faced with somewhat elusively. "Why all of this shadowboxing about the reality of God? Let us be plain with it: show us! Show us in a way that human beings can straightforwardly recognize, and it is enough. Show us in the way that we are constituted, that is, in a way that human beings can see ordinarily perceptible objects and ideas; let us see and we will believe; let us see and we can believe." This cry in its history reaches back to prophets and seers, even to Moses, who begged God in Exodus: "Show me thy glory" (Exod. 33:18).

"Show us" exemplifies the impatient, even despairing, voice: Have you not said that you are the way? That no one comes to the Father except through you (John 14:6)? That you are our access to God—the "place" of God? That you are the truth about God—and indeed, the

8. Carson McCullers, *The Heart Is a Lonely Hunter* (Boston: Houghton Mifflin, 1940), 50.

9. Jacques-Bénigne Bossuet, as cited in Henri de Lubac, *The Discovery of God* (Grand Rapids: Eerdmans, 1996), 115.

disclosure of God? Then show him to us now—and this is enough. It all seems so obvious, so plainspoken, so winning. All of this can be found in Philip's prayer: Show us God as you would anyone else. Let us see and experience God so that his reality is undeniable.

But notice what Philip's plea—this very human call—necessarily entails. It begs for God as object, rather than as subject. It allows for two alternatives, either of which entails its intrinsic contradiction. Either human beings re-create God as another human being and a product of nature—in a reductive practice that permeates the history of "religions"—so that he can be experienced in an obvious way open to any human being. Or they postulate some ecstatic object given by mysticism, *kenosis,* and rapture, far removed from what it means to be a human being. But either way—for all its attractive promise—is doomed to its intrinsic destruction. God is not to be advanced as another thing—as another object in the universe. Show him in that way, no matter how exalted the image or experience, and you have only created an idol. You will not have revealed God. You will have actually denied God. Neither alternative reaches the intrinsic transcendence of God. Neither way saves human life; both ways destroy it in its own finitude.

Can God only be revealed by his actual denial?

And yet, there is a way to connect these two, to mediate between the divine reality and the human, to incarnate the divine within the human or elevate the human into God. There is a way to link the divine and the human so that the human becomes a communication with the reality of God—so that the human becomes the word of God's reality, of God's presence and concern. It is not argument or inference. Argument seldom settles anything as deep as questions about the reality of God. Ambrose of Milan wrote, "It was not by dialectic that it pleased God to save His people" ("Non in dialectica voluit Dominus populum suum salvum facere").[10] Only an embodiment of the reality of God, as opposed

---

10. Ambrose of Milan, *De Fide* 1.5, in Migne, Patrologia Latina 16:537; En-

to argument, will definitively disclose his truth. It is only this witness that gives disclosure and hope.

This has been the constant claim of Christianity, that there must be mediation between God and human beings—otherwise one deals in falseness, abstractions, or pretensions. There must be a mediation that is true both to the infinite and to the finite, both to the unspeakable reality that is God and to the limited reality that is human. In this way, there must be a "place" where God can be found—to follow William of St. Thierry's metaphor. So we discover in 1 Timothy 2:5: "There is one God and there is one mediator between God and [human beings], the [human being] Jesus Christ."

It is true that everything bears witness to the reality of God, everything that is. "The world is charged with the grandeur of God,"[11] as Hopkins wrote. But the kind of knowledge that responds to the interpersonal longings of human beings for meaning and truth, and the interpersonal disclosure of God, cannot be satisfied by a God whom one only knows by inference, "a friend behind the phenomenon." The longing is personal; the fulfillment of that longing must be interpersonal.

It is in coming to Christ by authentic longing that one comes to God. For the reality of God is not "delivered" like an object; it is pointed to. One does not "lay hold of God" as one does another thing, as another finite object. One is drawn to God as the horizon of everything. When the Christian asks about the reality of God, the question must come out of the Christian's longing—longing for meaning, longing for truth, longing for holiness—and the Christian is answered with the life and presence of Jesus. Ultimately God is always subject.

In this Gospel pericope, Philip and the other disciples are not

---

glish version, *On the Christian Faith* 1.5.42, in *Nicene and Post-Nicene Fathers*, ed. Philip Schaff and Henry Wace, 2nd ser., vol. 10 (Peabody, MA: Hendrickson, 1995), 207.

11. This is the first line of "God's Grandeur," a poem by Gerard Manley Hopkins, SJ.

to look beyond Christ—they are to look at Christ. They are to see him. In seeing him, they are seeing the Father.

What on earth does that mean?

Jesus is in the Father: one with God. Jesus takes the meaning and the direction of his life from God. The Father is in Jesus; he is revealing himself in Jesus. He is expressing himself in Jesus, as human beings express themselves through their words. In fact, Jesus is the human expression of God. How? By the words he utters and by the deeds he does—above all, by what he is. The meaning and the truth about God is to be found in Jesus.

Where does one find this Jesus? Where is one found by him?

Where is that presence available today? Where is the "place"? Where can Dr. Delbende or Mick look for a new hope; where can the diplomats and the scientists look for a revolution and enlargement in their perspective; where can the intellectuals and the media elites look for a world beyond their world? What can deliver the hope that the Jesus of John's Gospel offers?

Finally, what brings Jesus into our history, that is, allows him to be a presence, an undeniable presence, in this place and in this time? Is there any human reality that extends Christ into the world, other than the church? What makes him present in such a way that we can touch and see? Is it not paradoxically the character of this sinful but holy church? What else could it be besides the church? Is this church then not concretely the body, the extension of Christ into our time, into our history? And do we not mean the church, not in its global extension or abstraction so much as in this particular, concrete community that we see and encounter, out of which the universal church is constituted? Is it not this community that makes Christ available to our culture, this particular, limited community in which and out of which the universal church is constituted?

The church, for all its sins and scandalous limitations, insists upon the reality of Jesus, even in its own confrontation and confusion. What else can make Christ available today, in his words and in his works, at this concrete time and this concrete place—but the community? What else can put the spirit of Christ into the interiority of human beings so that they can come to see God in Christ—but this community? Concretely, here, at this time and this place: the community. That is why Christianity insists that Christ left his disciples not a creed, nor only a book, but an actual concrete community. In a world that has become tired of words, is it not this community that either extends the reality of Christ into the world or effectively and intractably inhibits it?

I wonder if this is not a critical part of the challenge of the Christian vocation today—to continue to build the church, as a community that bears the reality of Christ into our world—a witness to the love that is the finite actualization, the presence of the Spirit of Christ. To be for the world "a place" where the presence of God is obvious and definitional. To be where the members of the community are called to show the effects of that Spirit in the charity, the love and fidelity, the forgiveness by which they live the gospel. This can make the presence of Christ and the mediation of the gospel possible.

The alternative is terrible: it would mean the disappearance of Christ from culture. If the church does not bear witness to the reality of God by the quality and intensity of its charity and its communal life, it will bear witness to his unreality. If Christian lives are not authentic, they will make God seem fake. And so the question of Jesus to Philip is a profound challenge to the way Christians live out their lives: "Do you not believe that I am in the Father and the Father in me?" (John 14:10).

⊰ 10 ⊱

"AND WHAT SHALL I SAY?
'FATHER, SAVE ME FROM THIS HOUR'?"

*"Now is my soul troubled. And what shall I
say? 'Father, save me from this hour'? No, for
this purpose I have come to this hour. Father,
glorify thy name."* (John 12:27–28)

Jesus Questions Himself

Our last century witnessed significant—even revolutionary—advances within American Catholic spirituality, both in its affective understandings and in the effective consequences of what it means to be Christian. A comprehensive passion for social justice and for the alleviation of human suffering has grown in the sensibility and in the urgencies of contemporary spirituality. Perhaps more than in previous centuries, these initiatives constitute recognizably an indispensable, faithful, and deepening union with God. The hunger for justice and the hunger for the experiential presence of God are merging in human consciousness; they are coming to constitute a profound unity, one that is substantially shaping the retrieval in Catholic spirituality of a new fullness. Monasteries, Catholic universities, urban parishes, secondary schools, and religious orders, as well as theologians, have contributed to this evolution, and are themselves significantly reshaped by it. All are judged increasingly in their Christian validity as a consequence of their contributions to it.

But in the ambiguity of every human development, there is also loss. "Christian pessimism"—the Rahnerian recognition of the codetermination of even great and good enterprises by the influences, deceptions, and hidden temptations of evil and perversion—insists upon the inescapable possibility of negativity: the pervasive and ineluctable threat of evil in anything finite, even in the holy, is not to be softened by superficial, unthinking, bourgeois enthusiasms. The garden that you cultivate may become the house you cannot occupy. The battle for security may issue in the mindless slaughter of the innocent. Advances in technology can render the wonders of nature sterile and distant. In the name of heady technological purposes, one can increasingly come to live in a barren and cruel world of instruments and manipulated objects. In great advances, there always exists the real possibility of human diminishment.

In no area is this diminishment more effective and more treacherous than in its appropriation of the fidelity and paradoxical scandal of the cross. A great deal is written enthusiastically today about religious self-development, accepting oneself, the importance of psychological soundness, the integration of the whole person, etc. Such undeniably and supremely healthy concerns tend to overwhelm any negative reserve that was insisted upon in previous decades. Some loss should be attended to here. For when the shadow of darkness and significant interior pain bear in upon lives whose spirituality is shaped almost exclusively by happy, contented, and positive emphases and expectations, suffering is not infrequently found to be unintelligible, even unbelievable. One can make no sense of it.

What is at issue here is not that human advances court their own error, but that the advances themselves are inescapably ridden with a hidden entropy, emptiness, and loss. In an ideologically optimistic world, obligations, disappointments, and reversals can be as shocking as they are unexpected. Any experience of real pain can trouble commitments. Marriage or the priesthood can be abandoned by those convinced that God would never call anyone to the searing interior anguish or desolation entailed by a fidelity to previous commitments, or when one is called to surrender to someone deeply loved.

But such experiences are also profoundly problematic for a contemporary meditation on the passion of Christ. To grasp the religious significance of this darkness, one can turn to the scene in the twelfth chapter triggered by the request of the Greeks and the question that Jesus proposes in his anguish.

Jesus realizes that the hour for his dissolution has come: "Now is my soul troubled. And what shall I say? 'Father, save me from this hour'? No, for this purpose I have come to this hour. Father, glorify thy name" (John 12:27–28).

The Gospel has raised many questions that Jesus directed to his disciples—for their consideration, for their comfort, for their challenge, for their assimilation, and for the redirection of their lives—questions that cry out to any disciple of Jesus for a response.

But here and now, it is radically different. The Gospel now has Jesus questioning not his disciples, but himself. He is searching himself at the very moment of the triumph of his mission. This is the decisive hour, the one for which he was made. His mission is here. He questions himself more as the reach of this mission becomes universal. But why here?

If one hears this question and interiorizes the way that Jesus responds, one may come to understand why the passion of Jesus worked human salvation, why one can say that Jesus died for our sins, why this suffering and passion make for the joy of the world and the glory of God. So much in human understanding here depends on how one appropriates Christ's revelation of suffering and fidelity.

Suffering and Its Continuities

Pain and suffering obviously contradict the satisfactions and confirmations conferred by pleasure. They contradict the expectations that go with a "happy life." Pleasure is spontaneously taken as a sign that "things are going well." Human beings make decisions on the direction of their own lives according to what they enjoy. One chooses in such a case, not according to the options and elements in this choice, but because of the quota of pleasure and satisfaction that is experienced or expected. Human beings expect pleasure to confirm the value and health of their choices. When pleasure is not forthcoming or when it evanesces, they draw back in pain; they recoil from such commitments. Suffering staggers the continuity of fidelity.

If human choice is to have any perduration, another motive must enter into its calculus and replace the absent pleasure or satisfaction that had supplied the previous motive for choice. What is good or valuable must in some way be done for its own sake, not because of the payback or recompense in other coin. Human beings call this attraction and its choice love. When this is the case, the strength of love promises continuity and depth. Such love does not depend on some more basic or retrograde motive. What is chosen, then, must be supported by this love. And when this love is God or the attributes of God or the effect of love, love takes on the character of the love of God. It becomes a form of the absolute presence of God.

Sin, classically, is the decision for the absence of God. It is a choice or a situation in either a personal or social world in which this absence is evoked or expected, even unthinkingly usual, taken for granted. Jesus was to die that this privation of God from human life would not become the usual, the chosen, the habitual, or the human condition. To say that Jesus died for our sins, for the forgiveness of sins, is to say that through the choice and obedience of Jesus, the Spirit of God would become in human life a renewed presence, an insistent presence, the contradiction and the eradication of the absence of God; it is to say that God would emerge in this love as the definitional presence in human lives. In the forgiveness of sins, the Spirit of God itself specifies who we are, supreme over all evil. Forgiveness is this renewal of the presence of God in his Spirit.

The passion in John, therefore, is not the defeat and destruction of Jesus, but his triumph over the absence of God. It is a triumph of God that this renewed presence of the Spirit breathes again into human actuality. Forgiveness is then the insistence that this presence of the Spirit of Christ removed, by its fullness, any absence of God. Forgiveness is then the renewed and specifying presence of God within the previous context of sin and denial.

The Passion of Christ

The passion of Christ opens with the experience of this absence and its privation. The Greeks—who enter as the whole non-Jewish world—come to the ever-available Philip. They were Greeks by their birth, not members of the chosen race—they were outsiders. They had moved out of a pagan culture into a kind of second-degree Judaism. Their plan to worship God at the feast implies that they belonged to the class known as "Godfearers," who were not allowed to share in the eating of the Passover lamb.[1] But even their minimal contact allowed them to hear of Jesus, to puzzle about him, to wonder about his life, and then finally to approach—not Jesus directly, but one who may have been the most approachable of the disciples, Philip—and to put their request with enormous reverence: "Sir, we wish to see Jesus" (John 12:21). How poignantly this request personalizes and specifies the first question of Jesus in the Gospel: "What do you seek?" (1:38).

---

1. Rudolf Schnackenburg, *The Gospel according to John*, vol. 2, *Commentary on Chapters 5–12* (New York: Seabury, 1980), 381.

These Greeks, in their religious ascent to this moment, embodied for the later Christian community the world's longing to see the promised Messiah. It is the climax of religious searching in the Johannine narrative, the hope of joy, the hope that there would be joy. Through it, the whole world changes. Gentiles are coming to Jesus—to Jesus mediated through the community of his disciples. What would become the mission and purpose of the church has begun—one can catch a sense of incipient completion or even exuberance in this text. Joy, writes Thomas Aquinas, is both the fulfillment of desire and the completion of love.

The Seed of Grain

But what response do these pagans receive? Seemingly no direct response—in fact, they disappear from the text—and yet Jesus's words were as profound and as paradoxical as he could author. What does he do? He takes the experience to another plane, to a sense of expectation. He talks of glory. He recognizes what is happening and what is to happen—that his life is now (in this request) reaching its climax, in his suffering and death, in its meaning for us and for the entire world. His hour has finally come—in a way that it had not come at Cana (John 2:4), or at the Feast of Tabernacles (7:6–30), or while teaching in the temple treasury (8:20). But in his response to the search and longings of these Gentiles, it does come. The divine presence within the world was reaching its apogee, its completion.

Jesus comes both at the end and at the beginning of a developmental inclusion that specifies all creation, one that reaches back to the very creation and origins of dynamic matter, all movement and time. Progressively God first prepared a world, then a human race to whom he could in Christ give not another thing but himself in the incarnation. The apostles were to foster the fulfillment and the radiance of this transformed world. Jesus in this way and in this conclusion is to allow the human race unparalleled access to God. And what will effect for him this "law of access"? What will constitute the salvation of the human race? Not another miracle, not another set of sermons, parables, and teachings. Only one thing will give Jesus access to God in such a way as to save the human race, and that is his utter surrender to God, his obedience unto death. For which reason "God has highly exalted him" (Phil. 2:9). For the union that was realized in his obedience, God gave him the power that no human had ever possessed, the ability to impart the Holy Spirit for the transformation of all human life. The Spirit was to constitute the new and specifying presence of God in human life. Jesus's death then was a response to the obedience asked by God: "Unless a grain of wheat falls into the earth and dies, it remains alone; but if it dies, it bears much fruit" (John 12:24). The cost would be himself.

But the passion? Why the passion? Let us not get unreal about the grain of wheat—it is cold, dark, and wet in the ground. The seed is itself alone. It gradually breaks apart, disintegrates, and out of this disintegration comes forth new life. So also for Jesus. His passion and death, his physical destruction, would paradoxically become his glorification. It is through his death that he would respond to the hunger of the world for life. This axiom will be the law of his life, making sense out of the Father's guidance: "If any one serves me, he must follow me; and where I am, there shall my servant be also" (John 12:26). It will also be the law for those who follow him, those who, like Philip and Andrew, would serve him. They must follow him into this way whose fullness only he would endure. But the last and final word even here is not death; it is glory.

But how can suffering, sorrow, and death glorify God? It is a question for Jesus, but it is also a question for us—for all Christians, haunted by the mystery of the meaning of suffering and death. What can be said before the contradictions of this moment? This is all contained in the question of Jesus, "What shall I say?"

Here it is crucial to recognize that God is endlessly present; God is always "there" for us. If God were not present, nothing would exist. The presence of God supports and sustains the reality of all things. But when that presence becomes so palpable, so "tangible" that a human being actually experiences something of it, then we talk not so much about the presence of God, but more about the glory of God. The glory of God is the life-giving, tangible, self-evident manifestation of the presence of God.

It is crucially important, then, to recognize that as Jesus moves into the passion, he changes; he is deepened in his obedience, in his union with God, deepened precisely because there was so much that counted or drove against it. One way love becomes successively deeper is that, as it is challenged, it gathers to itself all its resources to withstand or contradict the forces that bear in against it; as it faces opposition, it grows. Hebrews 5:8 actually speaks of Jesus as "learning obedience" through his sufferings. His suffering brings out what he is and also deepens it. His passion moves him to his resurrection. It is his triumph.

The choice and love demanded by the passion of Christ deepen the presence and the Spirit in Jesus's human life. His humanity thus becomes an instrument, a "sacrament," of that presence. This is his glorification, the intense and palpable presence of God.

Jesus is to be so open to the influence and direction of God, so obedient to the Father even unto death, that nothing could have a complementary influence over him. He gives his life over for this service in love. And the fulfillment is the purpose of it all: "For their sake I consecrate myself" (John 17:19). Jesus changed and deepened, as he learned obedience, as he was made complete and was sanctified.[2]

For which reason, God "exalted" him (Phil. 2), and gave him the intrinsic destiny and charge that no other human had ever re-

2. Raymond Brown, SS, *The Gospel according to John: I–XII,* Anchor Bible (Garden City, NY: Doubleday, 1966), 475.

ceived, to communicate the Spirit of God to all human beings. So it is, that to be in Christ is to be in and of the Spirit. This supreme gift of God to the obedient Jesus brings to its fulfillment the life and significance of Jesus. It is his mission. To bring him to this moment so that he became the incarnate source of the Spirit of God within the world: this is the comprehensive reason for which he lived and died, the fulfillment of everything he was. All the Gospels send the apostles forth with this injunction: baptize with the Spirit. But for this to happen, the seed had to fall into the ground and die, because the dying was the moment of Jesus's absolute choice of God.

How then does one respond to this question of Jesus, "What shall I say?" (John 12:27).

Out of the horror and its anticipation, Jesus asks himself about his entire prophetic mission: What shall I say? Now how shall he pray? What shall he say to God? He, who was always so sure, so certain about what he would do; he who knew that God always heard him (John 11:42); now in all this human weakness, he wrestles in his agony with this decision: What shall he say to God? Throughout the Gospel he had asked questions of others. Now Jesus asks a question of himself: "Now is my soul troubled. And what shall I say? 'Father, save me from this hour'?" (12:27).

It is the crisis of his mission—to die for the human race the death of the faithful and obedient prophet. But the agony that awaits him does evoke this cry spontaneously, this question—as it would in anyone who is faithful. Like Isaac Jogues, weeping the night before he goes to die; or like the terrified Blanche in *Dialogue of the Carmelites*.

But, in time and in grace, terror gives way to steely peace, to resolve—to trusting. Fear is not the end. Obedience in his life passes through to his fulfillment, as the bearer of salvation, of a new and unsurpassable presence of God.

While this is not a question of Jesus to us, but to himself, it is also to us and to every human being who would follow Jesus: "Where I am, there shall my servant be also" (12:26)—even to those who have been appointed to go and bear fruit that will remain (15:16). Every Christian is also caught up in this paradox of the "seed of grain." Every Christian, to be a Christian, is to follow Jesus's law of access, confident even in his fears, that the last word is God's. But this last word becomes paradoxically the promise of endless joy. What does this do, then, with suffering? Is not it to be experienced simply as loss? Something we must endure even though it is experienced as something that makes no sense and works endless terror? One must learn from Jesus the meaning and the possibilities, the strengths and the trust of living in obedient suffering without wavering in a fundamental confidence in the trustworthiness of God. It is in this trust, when all the human support has given way, that God becomes God in our lives: the absolute source and the support of all human life that is given to God when everything else is taken away.

ᴥ(11)ᴥ

"SHALL I NOT DRINK THE CUP
WHICH THE FATHER HAS GIVEN ME?"

Jesus said to Peter: "Put your sword into its sheath; shall I not drink the cup which the Father has given me?" (John 18:11)

The "Hour" from God and for God

The life of Jesus reaches its contradictory climax in the horror and the glory of his passion, death, and resurrection, in the great wonder of the "paschal mystery." Here, his governing, adamant longing for the salvation of the entire human race was realizing its native promise in his terrible suffering and agony, both mental and physical, permeated and specified by his love and obedience. This would climax in drawing all human beings to himself, dying upon the cross and rising from the dead. The Johannine Christ—Jesus in the interpretation of John's Gospel—was utterly conscious that this moment, this "hour" and everything about it, was *from God* and *for God*. This was the cup the Father had given him to drink. In all his suffering, even in death itself, there was a strange and haunting greatness.

This moment and its sufferings, the repudiations and agony, came not finally from the high priests, the Pharisees, and the Sanhedrin, nor from the Roman procurator and soldiers. They came from God, measures by which the strange and unfathomable providence of God would reach its purposes. This was the moment unsurpassable, the strange and paradoxical gift from the Father. For it would evoke the fidelity, the loving obedience, that was finally the gift of God and the transformation of Jesus that was his resurrection.

The thirteenth chapter opens precisely upon this conviction. Jesus knew that the Father had given all things into his hands, and that he had come "from God and was going to God" (John 13:3). His ministerial life was dominated by this tension. This was the pervasive claim of the passion and death upon his life: that God willed it. All this was in some remarkable, mysterious way the profound gift from God.

Fidelity to this dark guidance of God flooded and specified his work here. He was convinced that God called him to this moment, to this task. God asked him to undergo in terrible fashion the fate of the faithful prophet. In the Synoptics, with the agony in the garden, and in John, with the rebuke to Peter, Jesus expressed this fundamental consciousness and conviction: that God is in and above all, and finally at the origin and purpose of all that happens. Nothing stands outside the guiding hand of God. Hence his question to Peter, which human beings came to make their own as they would come to walk the path he opened for them: "Shall I not drink the cup which the Father has given me?" "*The Father has given me . . .*" What Jesus was realizing and accepting was—all of it—enveloped and made bearable within his profound and governing sense of a personal providence that guided every moment and every choice of his life. Few convictions stand in greater contrast with contemporary religious sensibility; hence, the pertinence of his question here to Peter.

Over the past centuries, a significant limitation found within Catholic theology and ordinary religious reflection has been the repudiation of, or opposition to, or skepticism about any substantial belief in such particular providence, that is, that God intimately cares for and provides for each person. Such a belief, once so pervasive and accepted as fundamental to Christianity, has been shaken to its foundations by the horrors of the twentieth century. After the suffering visited upon untold millions, can anyone with any seriousness and integrity believe or hope that God intervenes in and directs the world; that God actually governs the world in any real sense of that word; that human suffering in some sense is from him, or that he can or will do anything about it? Do human beings wait expectantly upon such an intervention or such care?

During these years of unimaginable cruelty, poverty, torture, and relentless oppression, Christian theologians have, paradoxically enough, judged that human beings have now come of age, that God has left human beings within the creative disposition of the universe, and that anything like a particular providence, a continual and personal interaction with God, is primitive or premodern—making God, as one of these theologians told me, more available to human beings than was the case. Indeed, prominent process theologians stressed an impersonal providence that lures human beings further into the future so that their choices eventually constitute the consequent nature of God.

The central religious question—one that permeates and possesses our times, one that enters into every facet of the human religious understanding of our world and of our place within it—the unavoidable question, however much people would avoid it, remains that of providence. For human beings are inescapably focused upon a divine and comprehensive presence, action, and guidance in the world, even when this exists in their lives only as a longing or denial.

Finally every human being finds himself or herself at some juncture in life asking this question in one form or another. Does it make any sense to hope that God or something in the mystery of life really cares for the fate, the destiny, the path of human beings? Does it make any sense to assert that God cares for me? What do

I see in my life that honestly grounds such a trust that God really effectively cares for the universe—and that God really cares for me? How does it make any sense to assert that God intervenes in human lives and guides them? Does God really intervene in the life of the church and guide it? How much can be made of those lilies of the field?

A conviction here is pivotal for a life of prayer, for a life of faith and personal union with God, and for an understanding of Christian spirituality. Many centuries ago, Aquinas wrote: "There is an obstacle to prayer or confidence in God that would deter one from praying. This is the notion that human life is far removed from divine providence."[1] The thought is given expression in the words of the evil person in Job 22:14: "Thick clouds enwrap him, so that he does not see, and he walks about the vault of heaven."[2] Before evil and suffering, assertions of a caring Providence can ring unreal: "He does not see." This constitutes the central religious problem in our times.

Providence and the Witness of the Saints

From this contemporary, even tortured discussion, one central source of theology has often been omitted, namely, the experience of the saints. That is doubly strange because contemporary theologians, such as Hans Urs von Balthasar and Karl Rahner, have stressed that the experience of the saints should enter constitutively into the cognitive content of Catholic theological thought.

---

1. Thomas Aquinas, *Compendium of Theology*, trans. Cyril Vollert, SJ (St. Louis: Herder, 1947), 322.

2. John of the Cross, "Letter 26: To Madre María de la Encarnación, discalced Carmelite in Segovia, July 6, 1591," in *The Collected Works of John of the Cross*, trans. Kieran Kavanaugh, OCD, and Otilio Rodriguez, OCD, rev. ed. (Washington, DC: Institute of Carmelite Studies Publications, 1991), 760.

This is also the contemporary assertion of such promising younger theologians as Richard Miller.[3]

Within such a set of coordinates, the theological reflection upon providence and the consequent theology built upon this would be remarkably different. The experience of the saints does not so much explain or justify the insistent evangelical reliance upon providence as it embodies it, gives it witness, intelligibility, and historical grounding. This witness does not so much substantiate how providence works as it provides a warrant that providence is, is everywhere present, and is all-pervasive. Here lies the basis for the reflections on providence that are religious—on the active presence and intervention of God—and a consequent theology built upon this as principal evidence. One does not so much look for an elaborate intellectual structure, a deductive theory of providence, or a metaphysics of the relationship of the world to God. One may rather take as its evidence in this dialogue the experience and sanity of the saints: their practice of absolute trust in God, their utter reliance upon God's guidance, their unconditioned search to discover the will of God for them, the surrender of themselves in a manner that contradicts a good deal of the easy dismissals of contemporary deism. All these constitute a massive challenge to contemporary theology. How is it possible and religiously feasible today to live out or to sustain this kind of confidence in the intimate and guiding hand of God? And how does one discern the vital presence and direction of this guidance? In the history of communities or of religious persons, how does one discern with any certainty the direction of this guidance? All these issues bear upon providence as this pivotal religious challenge of today.

Much of our Catholic theology of providence over the past

3. For further information, see Richard Miller, "The Eternal Plan of Divine Providence and the God Who Dialogues: The Contribution of John H. Wright, S.J.," in *Sacra Doctrina: Insights from Young Theologians*, ed. Anna Bonta Moreland and Joseph Curran, C21 Book Series, ed. James F. Keenan, SJ, and Patricia Deleeuw (New York: Herder and Herder, 2012), 165–93.

centuries has been "providence from above," an a priori doctrine. What needs to be formulated today is much more a "providence from below": the hope, attitudes, convictions, lives, and habits of the saints in their relationship with God. From these we can gather some indication of what the providence of God must be to have evoked and grounded such trust, such hope. Such a procedure would be to move from the fact to the "reasoned fact." What is there in the awareness of the saints that allows them to assert providence confidently and intimately?

Three very different examples might illumine what is meant by the experience and conviction of the saints. Shortly before his death in August 1591, a vicious movement arose against John of the Cross in the newly formed Vice-Province of the Discalced Carmelites. Stripped of his offices, John was exiled to the solitude of La Peñuela in Andalusia. He was even investigated by Fray Diego Evangelista in an effort to expel him from the order. By September the bacterial infection (erysipelas) that was to end his life had taken hold, and he was directed by his superior to go for further medical treatment. While all this storm was gathering around him, he wrote to the prioress of the nuns in Segovia: "Do not let what is happening to me, daughter, cause you any grief, for it does not cause me any. . . . Men do not do these things, but God, who knows what is suitable for us and orders things for our good. Think nothing else but that God orders all things—and where there is no love, put love, and you will find love" ("De lo que a mí toca, hija, no le dé la pena, que ninguna a mí me da. . . . No piense otra cosa sino que todo lo ordena Dios, y adonde no hay amor, ponga amor, y sacará amor").[4] That remains a stark and provocative conviction about providence: that in the last analysis it is not human beings who determine what enters our lives and forms the human situation, but God. God ordains all things, and God works in all things for

4. John of the Cross, "Letter to María de la Encarnación, Prioress of the Discalced Carmelites in Segovia," in *The Collected Works of John of the Cross*, 703.

our good; nothing is excepted. Saint Augustine is followed by Saint Thomas in his insistence that the goodness and power of God do not dictate that no evil exists. Such a necessity would eliminate human free choice—that the second state would be worse than the first. The goodness of God and the power of God are shown in that even out of evil God can draw a greater good.[5] It is this conviction that underlies the question of Jesus—"Shall I not drink the cup which the Father has given me?" (John 18:11).

This is not a pure passivity or a version of historical determinism, nor is it a mitigation or denial of human freedom and creativity. Human freedom, with its hopes and choices, is itself part of God's providence, not its contradiction. But when one can go no further concretely in resistance to evil or in the creativity of positively good initiatives, then one can find even in these irreducible facts the hand of God's providence, however cast in shadows. When one must undergo evil, then one accepts surrender to this providence as a dark but real part of God's individual care. Nothing is excised from this providence. Even here God remains sovereign Lord.

Thus, in the beginning of the seventeenth chapter of the third book of the *Imitation of Christ,* possibly the most influential religious book since the dawn of the *devotio moderna* and the volume carried constantly by Dag Hammarskjöld, one finds this exhortation of Christ to the reader:

Christ: Son, let me do what I choose with you: I know what is best for you. You think as a man: you decide in many matters as human feeling prompts.

Disciple: Lord, what thou sayest is true. Thy anxiety for me is greater than all the care I can take for myself. Most precariously he stands who does not throw all his disquietude upon thee.

5. Thomas Aquinas, *Summa Theologiae* I-II, 3, ad 1.

Lord, if my will keeps upright and strong towards thee, do with me whatever pleases thee.[6]

God is at work in all human beings and in all human history. When each person finds himself or herself caught up in that presence and guidance—however little understood—that person carries this divine activity faithfully into the world. This confidence or trust is finally the foundation for the surrender of all things unto God. Nothing supervenes or surpasses the comprehensive actions of God.

Reading, finally, through the letters of Ignatius of Loyola, one may be struck by what he wrote to a compulsive, overworked man of immense good will. Ignatius urges him toward greater moderation in his activity—and he does so out of his understanding and convictions about divine providence: "In the things that occur or will occur, it will be profoundly appropriate to hold yourself prepared to accept either of the two alternatives—that is to say, success or opposition—with a good will as from the hand of God. It is enough for us that we do what we can according to our own fragility and that we leave the rest to divine providence—whose concern it really is and whose ways of development human beings do not understand. For this reason they are sorrowful about things that happen about which they ought to rejoice."[7]

In all these examples of the saints, one finds in very different ways an understanding of providence that is close to what one finds in the simplicity of the Sermon on the Mount. Indeed, it is in this way that the Gospels contextualize the attitude of Jesus toward his passion. His attitude comes out of the profound and pervasive sense of the direct providence of God.

For providence is not a grand plan in which each detail of finite

6. Thomas à Kempis, *Imitation of Christ*, trans. Edgar Daplyn, FRSL (New York: Sheed and Ward, 1950), 94.

7. *Letters of St. Ignatius of Loyola*, trans. William J. Young, SJ (Chicago: Loyola University Press, 1959), 413.

reality is prescribed to a particular function or vocation. To think of it in these terms is to discredit it. The understanding of providence issues from the insistent conviction that God is at work in all things, acting in accordance with the constitution of each thing. In joy or in suffering, God offers us finally whatever comes into our lives. Even here, then, in everything, everything is gift.

Whatever human beings do with these gifts and whatever God does with the products of their freedom depend also upon this freedom. For God is preeminently free. And God asserts this freedom as he chooses to respond to the choices that human beings have made. Our human histories then will take the shape of the improvisations he effects. The providence and purpose of God will improvise and shape a response to human choice in the accomplishment of God's purpose within the universe. If one wants to specify the providence of God, one must insist that this providence has a comprehensive purpose that includes all things, and that God improvises with all the things he has made and governs in a nuanced way to achieve that purpose.

The question of Jesus to Peter arises within the events that follow Jesus's arrest. He has just secured the release of his disciples. Then Peter strikes off the ear of the high priest's slave, Malchus. The episode will be variously told in all four Gospels, and John uses it not out of interest in the disciples' resistance, but for the sake of the very last question that Jesus will put to Peter before the passion: "Put your sword into its sheath; shall I not drink the cup which the Father has given me?" (18:11).

God is at work—even here. Jesus discerns that providential working and its enigmatic gifts, and tries, in spite of great repugnance, to accept or cooperate. Jesus is convinced that God has "handed him over." Peter, as usual, simply does not understand the destruction of Jesus and reacts typically according to his lack of understanding. T. S. Eliot was keenly conscious of how easily and how often we repeat the opaqueness of Peter—how Peter is not he, but us! So his poem "Ash Wednesday" turns to the Virgin, the symbol also of the church, and prays both to Our Lady and also perhaps for the church:

> Blessed Sister, holy mother,
>> spirit of the fountain, spirit of the garden,
> Suffer us not to mock ourselves with falsehood
> Teach us to care and not to care
> Teach us to sit still
> Even among these rocks,
> Our peace is in His Will.[8]

"His will." But unlike Peter—unlike us—Jesus does discern, understand, and trust the movements of providence in his life, that God is here at work: the Father has extended to him the cup of death, but the action of Jesus is toward human beings. This is a moment not for understanding but for surrender. So Schnackenburg can write: "Jesus not only surrenders to the Father's Will, but takes it over with total conviction."[9] This unifies his entire life and spells out all his integration of all things into divine providence.

Contemporary astrophysics recognizes something similar in our universe. Gravity brings together the very disparate and massive galaxies, so as to form the stars and the planets in their internal unity and external structures. So, in the Gospel of John, the will of God pervades the universe like gravity. It is this that effects providence, the intrinsic order by which God orders the universe and draws it to God's own self. Providence brings into unity and coherence all the disparate and contradictory elements in human life—all the chaos and the malice and the sin and the mistakes yield finally to providence.

It is appropriate then to see how in these short verses the sixth

8. T. S. Eliot, "Ash Wednesday," in *The Complete Poems and Plays, 1909–1950* (San Diego: Harcourt, Brace & Co., 1971), 67.

9. Rudolf Schnackenburg, *The Gospel according to John*, vol. 3, *Commentary on Chapters 13–21* (New York: Crossroad, 1982), 227.

chapter of John echoes in the question to Peter: "All that the Father gives me will come to me; and him who comes to me I will not cast out. For I have come down from heaven, not to do my own will, but the will of him who sent me; and this is the will of him who sent me, that I should lose nothing of all that he has given me, but raise it up at the last day. For this is the will of my Father, that every one who sees the Son and believes in him should have eternal life; and I will raise him up at the last day" (John 6:37–40). Now all this teaching comes to its moment of truth, to its climax at the hour when he is to die—the way that all human values and choices are clarified in the moments of pressure and crisis.

The agony is before him. Many voices are around that threaten. The clumsy attempt of Peter is to save him.

So in all this, the question that embodies and summarizes his life challenges ours. Jesus sees what is happening as coming from the Father, and so he asks the question: "Shall I not drink the cup which the Father has given me?" (18:11).

〜(12)〜

"DID I NOT TELL YOU THAT IF YOU WOULD
BELIEVE YOU WOULD SEE THE GLORY OF GOD?"

> *Jesus said, "Take away the stone." Martha,
> the sister of the dead man, said to him, "Lord,
> by this time there will be an odor, for he has
> been dead four days." Jesus said to her, "Did
> I not tell you that if you would believe you
> would see the glory of God?"* (John 11:39–40)

A Confrontation with Death

This question in John guided the disciples into the meaning and staggering comprehensive hope that Jesus offers. This question catches up the purpose of everything that has gone before: the resurrection and eternal life to which human beings are called, the meaning and the purpose of Jesus, his resurrection in glory. Jesus is to be fulfillment and destiny. He promises this and realizes it in his gift of the indwelling Spirit of God as the climax and the completion of his life, death, resurrection, and ascension. The contradiction of this promised glory with the death that is all around him could not be more stark.

The context of Jesus's question to Martha is death. Death, as something that had been dreaded, is first noticed as coming on inexorably: an illness; a growing anxiety; frantic prayers to Jesus, with no response and no presence; only an experience of silence and absence. His silence is like the dark silence of God. Those who had followed him in trust are now alone with the dying. The death comes with wrenching sadness and emptiness. It is accepted, as one must accept death, with desolate friends with their mourning, and long, endless days after the burial.

And now it is over: accepted and settled—a searing memory, but now only a memory. There is a terrible sense of loss—their brother had died—but also a sense, even more terrible, of being lost; there had been no answer from Jesus. But at last, it is over, for Mary and Martha and the crowd of friends, and even for his disciples—for he goes to the graveyard, the tomb of his friend, and weeps. In the same way that Luke would have him weep over the irrevocable doom of Jerusalem (Luke 19:41), and Hebrews would have him weep over his own approaching death (Heb. 5:7).

Then, in this sorrow and resignation—as he could not for Jerusalem and would not for himself—he intervenes: "Roll back the stone." Martha is horrified that this squalor would be added to what they have suffered already—that this would be her last memory of their brother. And then—to her agony and uncomprehending emptiness, Jesus places this question, the last that he will pose in the Johannine public ministry: "Did I not tell you that if you would believe you would see the glory of God?" (John 11:40).

John's Gospel records that Jesus had said that "the hour is coming, and now is, when the dead will hear the voice of the Son of God, and those who hear it will live. . . . The hour is coming when all who are in the tombs will hear his voice" (5:25, 28). But that was a word, a promise, a few sentences, talk. This is stark death and loneliness and endless ache—an experience that one lives with and sleeps with, that one cannot escape all the waking moments of the day.

But what does that promise and reality come to now? This is the terrible experience of sheer, agonizing contradiction—the promise in the reality—the promise in spite of the reality—the promise . . . while everything around makes that promise seem so hollow and empty.

But what is Martha to do? To cling to the promise and deny

the reality would be madness. But to deny the promise because the reality is overwhelming would be faithlessness. Is she to hold on to both: to endure and to wait, when waiting seems the most impossible of all? Martha is called to hope, and "hope that is seen is not hope" (Rom. 8:24).

Martha stands for every person who has ever committed himself or herself to Jesus, who has understood him as the meaning and anchor of life, only to have lost everything—in a graveyard of emptiness and of ruined expectations.

The Paradox of Christian Hope

This is the great paradox of Christian hope. The actual experience of hope and the actual experience of despair are very often the same experience. "Hope that is seen is not hope" (Rom. 8:24). It may be animal enthusiasm, optimism, social buoyancy, the attitude that "things are going well"—but it is not hope. And yet it is not the experience of despair, although the experience is that no hope is to be seen.

The radical difference between hope and despair will not be illumined by the experience; it is caught up in the words and promise of Jesus: "If you would believe . . ." Belief: the difference between hope and despair is not in the sensible experience nor in social confirmation. It lies in the steady confidence and commitment in the promise of Jesus, the grace and commitment called faith. The choice is Martha's, a choice that again and again will confront anyone who has become involved with Jesus or the church or any priest or religious community, and has met the stunning contradictions of experience, betrayal, and death. Anyone who has encountered profound sinfulness, insensitivity, or arrogance in such a community inescapably confronts the question whether to continue, whether to hope in any very real way, or to despair.

And hope in what? In what does one believe, in the graveyard before the tombs? That "you would see the glory of God"? The glory of God? What can that possibly mean here? How much more difficult it is for Martha now than for the apostles at Cana; there Jesus first manifested his glory, and they had believed. Now it was much more difficult. He was calling first for an absolute commitment and trust, in spite of his absence and neglect of her prayers—in spite of no answer and the anxious waiting, in spite of the absurdity of the request, the shocking command that the grave be opened after death. In spite of all this, she is to believe and to hope: the naked, unsupported act of entrustment.

The great seventeenth-century spiritual theologian Jean Grou placed the question that emerges like a cry at this point: "But how far are we to carry this trust in God? As far as his power and his goodness, as far as our weakness and our own misery; that is to say, our trust is to be boundless."[1] What Christians are called to believe in is the gracious power of God that works in spite of all human expectations, that effects the resurrection from the dead. Not resuscitation, but resurrection. That God will transform and renew all things and give them new life. In this faithful trust emerge the triumph and the glory of God. Life from the dead uniquely manifests the infinite power of God in which Christians trust.

The future of Martha's faithful trust was to see the glory of God found in the resurrection of Christ and in the gift of the Spirit. Emptiness and failure and death were not to be the last word. God is the last word. And that word is life—that all will be changed into life by the Spirit of God. The final human reality for which human beings have been created and in which they are to be saved is joy—the completion of love. So Martha is to see the glory of God. It is in joy that Martha and all human beings are called to find this glory of God: the resurrection, the ascension, and the Spirit of God working this transformation.

1. Jean Grou, SJ, *Manual for Interior Souls* (London: Burns, Oates and Washbourne, 1892), 247.

All Christians must in some way live through this question to Martha. It brings to focus and purpose so much of their lives. Christian discipleship takes its meaning and value as human beings grasp already in their lives what Jesus has promised. Discipleship can only take its continuity, its fidelity, and its joy as Christians are held in the Spirit by this promise. The disciple lives by the promise and power of Jesus, and finally in the gift of the Spirit. This is his hope.

Catholics must recognize further that full novitiates; crowded convents and churches; security and resources; confidence from the week's success, from the favorable opinions of others, from the applause of our motives, will eventually fail. Either because the crowds will walk away, or because the work will seem to demand more than our resources can sustain, or because of the scandal and betrayal of the gospel by those who should minister to the gospel, or because we are called to suffer injustice and failure—the cross, the experience of Romans 8:18–25—or because of our own blindness. But this alone makes the gift of the Spirit possible.

As with Martha, so with every Christian: When the interior resources fail or cease to distract, the central question is placed before the grave: Can we, by the power of God, live faithfully in hope? Can we live in the hope that the resurrection is the final and definitive judgment of God? That God is our God? That we will see his glory? That in that glory we would reach the completion of our final and lasting joy? That the great hope of the psalmist would be answered even in our lives?

> As for me, I shall behold thy face in righteousness;
> when I awake, I shall be satisfied
> with beholding thy form. (Ps. 17:15)

And so the haunting question of Jesus in the graveyard—"Did I not tell you that if you would believe you would see the glory of God?"

⟨ 13 ⟩

"DO YOU TAKE OFFENSE AT THIS?"

Many of his disciples, when they heard it,
said, "This is a hard saying; who can listen
to it?" But Jesus, knowing in himself that
his disciples murmured at it, said to them,
"Do you take offense at this? Then what if you
were to see the Son of man ascending where
he was before? It is the Spirit that gives life,
the flesh is of no avail." (John 6:60–63)

The Inadequacy of Belief

Those whose faith had been staggered in this passage—so shaken
that they would walk with Jesus no more—were not the Pharisees
nor the various official types that John calls "the Jews." Those who
were moving away were his disciples, men and women who by
choice and call were habitually to be with him. Initial rhythms
of belief give way to unbelief, conferring a dialectical character
upon this crucial event. The entropy of a decaying enthusiasm
is here lodging in the very heart of his community of disciples.
Tested among these men are now the paramount centrality and
credibility of Jesus, and what was to become its eucharistic em-

bodiment. In mysterious ways this narrative articulates and studies the inadequacy, even the disintegration, of belief: the eclipse of the self-interested belief awakened by the feeding of the five thousand, the belief over the powers of nature evoked by the walking on water, and even the shattered belief before the claims of the eucharistic discourse. At Jesus as Messiah, that is, at Jesus as mediating the absolute character of the absolute God, the "Jews" had murmured and disputed among themselves. But at Jesus as mediated in the Eucharist, it is the disciples themselves—the community around Jesus—who murmured and left him. It is they who find the statement about Jesus invincibly "hard." Their God—even in his prophetic presence—was paradoxically too small for that littleness, too finite to be warrant for that faith he was claiming from human frailty.

Such are the waves that break inevitably over almost all serious religious experience. Human beings spontaneously diminish the constitution of God, the magnitude of God, the mystery of God; idols must be finite in order to claim credibility. The divine must be whittled down to human size and sensibilities. To have any possession of human imagination and understanding, God must fit into the usual human worlds with Safeway, *Time* magazine, and petty expectations. The human imagination must not be expected to bear up under the radical claims and dimensions of a providential God, that he could care for and govern each single person among the billions of worlds from the galaxies to the subatomic. It shakes the human imagination to confront such transcendence. It is utterly, unimaginatively beyond our experience. Human beings recognize that these claims are excessive, that no one could do this. So Jesus must not do it, and cannot be expected to do it either—no matter what has been said about sparrows falling to the earth and lilies of the field. To be humanly credible, Jesus must always act in or be reducible to a world of common sense with a "realism" basically like any other human figure. So human beings will necessarily project a God, a limited God, in their own human image, the human being writ very large and easier to sound out. This sensibility and conviction lie at the heart of both classical and modern paganism, and it eliminates any hope of an incarnation.

I have a friend—Tom Weston—a Jesuit priest who works with alcoholics, a dedicated man, much loved and very successful in his care for others. Many of those he works with have bitter stories to tell about the church or about harsh experiences with parents or priests and nuns in grammar school. Tom can listen, and listen sympathetically, for hours. But often his comment to them after hearing their histories will come down to this: "But I am talking to you about God. And God is much bigger than this. God is really big. Really Big!" The transcendence embodied in this limitless care, in this service, or in any inspiration toward authentic Christian living is always inescapably God, so infinite as to be incomprehensible, absolute mystery. "Your God is too small," too small to accommodate the reality of providence. The mystery of God is not that he is unintelligible, but rather that he is so intelligible as to be incomprehensible. To call upon the distinction that Saint Bonaventure insists upon, human beings can apprehend God or know God, but not comprehend him. It is the great paradox of Christianity that we are called to know God, who is incomprehensible.

It is necessary for human beings to be repeatedly called back to this prophetically—"*God is always greater, no matter how much we have grown.*"[1] Only this makes sense of the promise in which they live and to which they are called. It counters the tendency of all human beings to remake God in their own image—in their own little image. Christians must return again and again to Christ as the mysterious Word that is the expression of the limitless God. Otherwise, all their thoughts become disastrously too limited and mythological.

No one has devoted a greater portion of his writings to countering the tendency to shape or confine and so to minimize God, I suspect, than John of the Cross. One should not make, he insisted,

---

1. Augustine, "Expositions on the Psalms (Psalm 63)," in *Nicene and Post-Nicene Fathers*, ed. Philip Schaff, vol. 8 (Grand Rapids: Eerdmans, 1989), 262.

an absolute out of even the most intense religious experiences. They are and remain irreducibly finite: "however elevated God's communications and the experiences of His presence are, and however sublime a person's knowledge of Him may be, these are not God essentially, nor are they comparable to Him. . . . Regardless of all of these lofty experiences, a person should think of God as hidden and seek Him as one who is hidden."[2] God is always greater. No matter what the sublimity of one's thoughts and aspirations, God is always greater, infinitely greater.

Many years ago, while teaching theology at the Jesuit School of Theology at Berkeley, I was party to multiple conversations about the reality and the presence of God. The issue was often framed sharply in terms of two alternatives: substance or process. One incident I remember particularly was when a scholastic came up to me after class and protested that he could get very little out of theology courses. "I find them very confused and contradictory," he stated. "But one especially brought any hope for coherence in theology to a halt." He was speaking of the current debate whether God should be understood basically as substance or as process. His professor was teaching a theology influenced by the conceptual structures of Whiteheadian philosophy, while, on the other hand, strong voices also spoke for God as substance. The incongruity of the urgency with which the problem was regarded was stark. For human beings are called to worship the God who is finally beyond the limitations of substance or process—immensely useful as either might be in speculation in certain intellectual circumstances. Definitions and structures of thought point to the One who is utterly transcendent. Neither substance nor process as philosophically delineated can conceptually capture the reality of God. Both can point to the reality of the One who is transcendent, who grounds such a

2. John of the Cross, "The Spiritual Canticle," in *The Collected Works of John of the Cross*, trans. Kieran Kavanaugh, OCD, and Otilio Rodriguez, OCD, rev. ed. (Washington, DC: Institute of Carmelite Studies Publications, 1991), 479.

reflection, but God is always infinitely greater. This does not mean that one cannot know God. It does mean that what one knows is the always transcendent God as mystery, as infinitely intelligible.

As long as one does not fixate on such experiences, John argues, one should not be amazed that God calls human beings to a deep contemplation and transformation into him in love, even to an experience of God in love. Why not? "There is no reason to marvel at God's granting such sublime and strange gifts to souls He determines to favor. If we consider that He is God and that He bestows them as God, with infinite love and goodness, it does not seem unreasonable."[3] God is divine in the generosity with which he gives "infinite love and goodness."

"Does anyone take offense at this?" Jesus asked his disciples. Anyone seeking or longing for God must realize in utter humility first of all that God *is* God—and will always be infinite Mystery—the unspeakable Mystery of life that has bent over our lives in love: "Who alone has immortality and dwells in unapproachable light, whom no man has ever seen or can see" (1 Tim. 6:16). Second, he or she must realize that God *acts* as God: "At work within us [and] able to do far more abundantly than all that we ask or think" (Eph. 3:20). It is terribly misguided to set limits to the fulfillment of God's promises and providence or to fix boundaries to our confidence in his work in our lives. Human beings stammer as God approaches them: "Boundless love and goodness"; God—Utter Mystery—infinitely and pervasively present and at work in their lives.

The Trinitarian Glory of God

This sixth chapter of John climaxes in the presentation of Jesus as the bread of eternal life. The narrative begins with the symbolic

3. John of the Cross, "The Living Flame of Love," in *The Collected Works of John of the Cross,* 638–39.

feeding of the five thousand, and develops through the revelation of the power of Jesus over all nature, and finally concludes with the explanation of that feeding and of that power in the great discourse of the next day. The discourse itself develops from the summons to draw near to Jesus in faith—the bread of life—to the sacramental realization of this imperative. This is indeed stunning: that Jesus, and Jesus in his eucharistic presence, would be so central to human life.

Those who murmured at the transcendent and comprehensive centrality that Jesus comes to claim, murmured also at its eucharistic realization. At this murmuring, Jesus—as previously with Nicodemus—does not retreat from his positions or replace them. He rather increases their demands. In fact, he contrasts all that has been said with a still greater question that comes out of the question of this chapter: "Do you take offense at this? What if you were to see the Son of Man ascending to where he was before?" Under question are the ascension, the resurrection, and the exaltation of Jesus—what John will refer to as the glory that he had with the Father before the world was made (John 17:5). The central question of this entire chapter, the fulfillment and life of Jesus, is about the glory of God that Jesus shares with the Father and the Spirit—the Trinitarian glory of God.

This is the Jesus who is the full realization of what it means for God to give himself to us in Jesus Christ. The vision of God in Jesus is the destiny for which human beings were made. When you see Jesus, you see the promise of God for all human beings. "And this is eternal life, that they know thee, the only true God, and Jesus Christ whom thou hast sent" (17:3). God and Jesus Christ— they are one in the experiential knowledge that is eternal life. In the ascension of Jesus, the unity of Father and Son is disclosed to those who are possessed by the Spirit. Should the disciples not look forward to this vision? This is the purpose for which they were made, even though everything else will be left behind. This contemplation—and this fulfillment through death—is the vision of God, God revealed in Jesus Christ. It is here that Jesus introduces the purpose and completion of the human person. For here, as elsewhere, you become what you know.

This destiny is the bearing of the question. The logic of the question reveals the reality of God to be disclosed, revealed in Jesus. The question is the hermeneutic of everything that has gone before. So Schnackenburg comments that "Jesus' reply is deliberately phrased in the form of a question. He wants to make His hearers think further about His identity."[4] It is not just the Jews or the disciples—anyone who takes this question seriously cannot help but find it staggering. It is almost unthinkable that God has approached us—is approaching us—in this human being. It cannot even be thought without grace—without our being drawn by the Father. God is God—God acts as God—and he has chosen to come to us as a human being. The question of Augustine is: "Quid tibi sum ipse—ut jubeas te amari a me?" ("What am I to you, that you have commanded me to love you?").[5] What am I to you? This is the great question in which human beings are brought before God, and it comprehends all the questions of the Gospel of John.

Thus this question of Jesus in the sixth chapter—strangely enough—relativizes everything else that this chapter has contained, that is, it brings it to completion. It relativizes the physical feeding of the five thousand, the care for those in the storm and the claim *ego eimi*, the giving of himself as the source of eternal life, the realization of this gift in the Eucharist. All these are preparatory to seeing (*theorein*) the Son of Man ascending to where he was before—because this vision is eternal life. It was for this that we were made: our own completion in the exaltation of Jesus—the great hope for which we were born. Beyond all projection—the endless, infinitely loving mystery that we call Father.

4. Rudolf Schnackenburg, *The Gospel according to John*, vol. 2, *Commentary on Chapters 5–12* (New York: Crossroad, 1980), 71.

5. Augustine, *Confessions*, trans. Henry Chadwick (New York: Oxford University Press, 2009), 5.

The Inexhaustible Transcendence

What Jesus has asked again in this question is not something that human beings can answer. Like the questions "What are you looking for?," "What is this to you and to me?," "Do you know what I have done to you?," or "Do you love me?," there is no answer to this question. There is a response, however, and it is in the inexhaustible commitment of faith to the One who has loved us. The response embodies the mystery of God, encompassing the mystery of a human being, the question that God himself is for human life.

So it is not a problem that we consider—it is a question that we live with, an abiding hope that is a daily part of our lives—pointing us into the mystery that we serve and for which we long and for which we were made; but one that we do not yet see and one that we are always tempted to reduce, to make manageable. It is this question that keeps us from making our God too small. Above all, perhaps, it is a question that probes for a love that is greater than all that we can ask or think (Eph. 3:20), a vision and a love for which we were made: to live only "by the drawing power of his love and the voice of his calling!"[6]

Toward the end of his life, Karl Rahner was asked to address a conference of humanists at Salzburg—a meeting composed of scientists and philosophers, futurologists and historians. Before this immensely learned group, Rahner commented:

> All your cares, all your fears, all your exertions, your futurological optimism and pessimism, your heights and your depths, your triumphs and your defeats, are ultimately pointless and doomed to destruction, unless in this whole history there occurs that one love in which we forget ourselves for God, love Him for His own sake, adore Him; unless we succeed in living in an irreversible

6. *The Cloud of Unknowing*, ed. James Walsh, SJ (New York: Paulist, 1981), 117.

and inexhaustible transcendence to God, with no prospect of a return. Christianity stubbornly proclaims that happiness, quality of life, a better or a sound future for the world, for mankind, are not the ultimate, obvious standard values governing our actions; and, if they are made such, will lead us into eternal ruin. Christianity knows that to will one's own reality, to be intent on self-development and to seek happiness, are legitimate enterprises and that this determination, even if it has not yet been transformed into a radical love of God for His own sake, is not for that reason alone sinful and hostile to God. But Christianity stubbornly insists that only the love of God for His own sake will save us in the end.[7]

This is the call of this question: What is the hope in which we live? What is the love that is responsive to the questions of Jesus? What gives meaning to our Christian life and even joy to our death? Or have we made God too small—too distant—too distant because too small? "What if you were to see the Son of Man ascending to where he was before?"

7. K. Rahner, "The Inexhaustible Transcendence of God and Our Concern for the Future," in *Theological Investigations*, vol. 20, *Concern for the Church*, trans. Edward Quinn (New York: Crossroad, 1981), 177.

⤜(14)⤛

"IF IT IS MY WILL THAT HE REMAIN UNTIL
I COME, WHAT IS THAT TO YOU?"

*"If it is my will that he remain until I come,
what is that to you? Follow me!"* (John 21:22)

A Rebuke and a Question

A gentle but remarkable reciprocity attends the presence, the hopes, and the influence of great religious leaders and movements. A subtle reverence pervades the lives they inspire and permeates the atmosphere they foster. This effective presence transmutes into holiness those elements of life and personal histories that seem mutually exclusive: the determined and the flexible, the contemplative and the active, the abstractly metaphysical and the concretely practical, the sympathetic and the dogmatic. Their interchange continues to enrich and to specify the life of the church. For in very hidden ways, they are actually drawn into unique and abiding configurations by the spirit they communicate. One should hesitate, however, to formulate for each of these great traditions the actual spirituality that inspires and defines it. To determine such parameters could well be to miss in this greater clarity and abstraction the subtleties and the delicacy of the lived experience.

The Ignatian and Carmelite traditions, for example, seemingly so different, lay great emphasis upon the profound reverence—the almost eremitic quiet—that is to characterize much of their religious formation and practice. The kind of prayer to which they are habituated and the lengthy silence they foster are instantiated at critical moments, whether one is engaged in the thirty days of the *Spiritual Exercises* or the evening liturgical office. Jean Beyer, the great Belgian authority on secular institutes, judged solitary reverence so emphatic a note of Jesuit life that one could understand the Society of Jesus as the Carthusians made apostolic.[1] Perhaps something like this caution and insistence upon nuance lies behind the directions of so many founders, that outside of the structures of obedience, members do not try to direct or manage the lives of others. For no one can competently understand the mysterious direction of the spirit nor the hidden destiny of another person. Solitude reaches its personal fulfillment in the silence and hiddenness of that life, and so the religious rule does not contradict but embodies the claim of Paul that "your life is hid with Christ in God" (Col. 3:3). It is so with every Christian life lived at its depth: the religious claim upon a human life is very personal, subtle, and mysterious. At this deep level, one person's knowledge of another is at best a *docta ignorantia*.

The *Cautelas* of John of the Cross frame a classic treatment and one of the strongest and most uncompromising assertions of the call to this solitude. He gathers this experience into a renunciation, into a starkness that is hard to exaggerate:

> The third precaution is very necessary that you may know how to guard yourself in the community against all harm that may arise in regard to the religious. Many, by not observing it, not only have lost the peace and good of their soul, but have fallen and ordinarily continue to fall into many evils and sins.

---

1. For a fuller treatment, consult Michael J. Buckley, SJ, "Mission in Companionship: Of Jesuit Community and Communion," *Studies of the Spirituality of Jesuits* 11, no. 4 (September 1979): 14.

It is that you very carefully guard yourself against thinking about what happens in the community, and even more against speaking of it, of anything in the past or present concerning a particular religious; nothing about his character or his conduct or his deeds—no matter how serious any of this seems. Do not say anything under the color of zeal or of correcting a wrong—unless at the proper time to him by right you ought to tell. Never be scandalized or astonished at anything you happen to see or hear of, endeavoring to preserve your souls in forgetfulness of all that.

For, should you desire to pay heed to things, many will seem wrong, even though you may live among angels, because of your not understanding the nature of them.[2]

The *Cautelas* have their own strange and demanding idiom. But so much of this transposes the questions of Jesus in the Gospel of John to a definitive location within the abnegation and great promise of the resurrection. The Christian does not know what this providential care of God will demand, nor what particular destiny God has prepared for him or her. It is enough that the mysterious God calls and summons. The response must be one of total entrustment.

Hence the rebuke and question to Peter: "If it is my will that he remain until I come, what is that to you? Follow me!" (John 21:22). Religious men and women do not know the destiny or path that God has prepared for them. In this way they share in the mystery of Christ. The resurrection of Jesus and his second coming reveal not only who Christ is, but also who every human being is and, indeed, what the world itself is. The resurrection is the diaphony of all human life and history. One cannot understand human life,

2. John of the Cross, "Against the World: The Third Precaution," in *The Collected Works of John of the Cross*, trans. Kieran Kavanaugh, OCD, and Otilio Rodriguez, OCD, rev. ed. (Washington, DC: Institute of Carmelite Studies Publications, 1991), 721.

or even the life of Jesus, except in the light of the disclosure that is the resurrection. This coming of Christ is the final revelation of all things to every disciple.

The question of Jesus to Peter is a stark rebuke and correction—and the episode follows the typical pattern of Peter's life. Every time Peter is given a position of responsibility in the Gospels, it is followed by a correction and a stinging rebuke. The new position of responsibility and leadership seems to embolden Peter into a conviction of his unique and comprehensive importance, that his history and his person are the revelation of the meaning of it all. So that he, to whom the keys of the kingdom of heaven were to be given, would presume in his better judgment to counsel Jesus against the passion. So that he who would confirm his brothers, would boast that he would never betray Jesus. So that he, now so newly forgiven and uniquely singled out for the mission of the church, could ask for an account about the divine plan for others. Peter obviously felt entitled to pose this question. He had a right to know. There should be no secrets, no unknowns about others for someone like him.

Jesus answers his question with a question. "If it is my will that he remain until I come, what is that to you?" (21:22).

Peter's Unity Restored

His is a strange question, the last that Jesus will pose in the Gospel. It seems hauntingly so much like what is found in the marriage feast of Cana. Once more Jesus asks something along the lines of "What is this to me and to you?" The Gospel narrative opens with that question to Mary and closes with this question to Peter: "What is it to you?" Now the rehabilitation of Peter is to be complete—a rehabilitation that Jesus would bring to its conclusion with the summons "Follow me." The unity after the betrayal has been restored.

But Peter's attention is diverted from Jesus to his context among others. The Gospel says that Peter turned and saw the Beloved Disciple following them—and so much in the conversation changed.

Earlier in Matthew's narrative, Peter "got out of the boat and walked on the water and came to Jesus" (Matt. 14:29), that is, until he averted his gaze to the lake he was walking upon, to his context, and saw the wind, became afraid, and began to sink. On the lake it was fear; now, by the lakeshore, it was more than curiosity. It was the desire to understand how all these factors in their lives would now fit together; more precisely, how Jesus's arrangement of the destiny of his own life would work itself out in the destiny, the providence, of others. Peter had been forgiven, his future death foretold, and he had received the command to follow Jesus. Now, how about the other—the Beloved Disciple? There were still pieces to be put into place, and it seemed urgent that these pieces unite and harmonize.

In the Gospel of John, John and Peter had been linked at the Last Supper. There, Peter had signaled John to inquire who Jesus knew would betray him (John 13:23–24). Together they had run to the tomb, and the Beloved Disciple deferred to Peter's entering first (John 20:2–10). Everything in Peter must have wondered what would happen to him—what would govern or determine the mystery of his life. And so Peter put his question to Jesus, and Jesus's response was a question about his question. This is Jesus's last question in the Gospel of John, and it is a question that raises yet again the mystery of providence: "And if I wish that he remain until I come, what is it to you? You follow me!"

The question probes for the interiority of Peter, for what he knows and does not know, for what will have meaning and not have meaning. It directs Peter to look back upon himself and to find the shape and the direction that grace is taking in his life. Only this kind of graceful discernment will enable Peter to assimilate the last directive that Jesus gives him: to follow it with integrity and fidelity—all the days of his life. Unless Peter is aware of the directive presence of the spirit of Jesus within himself and can trust utterly that guidance with the entirety of his life, this imperative is simply impossible, in fact it is unintelligible. So this question about providence and all the future deepens into a question about absolute trust.

"Follow Me"

A number of commentators take this question of Jesus as directed to Christians at large. They divert the question back to us: "You are not to be concerned that you may die or suffer martyrdom while another lives until the parousia; your one calling is to follow me no matter where that following may lead you."[3] This captures the crucial point. For Peter's question was not about himself but about another. And it is from this that Jesus diverts him: "If I wish that he remain until I come, what is that to you?" That man is not under your management, your comprehension. He has his own mystery and his own solitude. Reverence it. Peter is called to recognize and respect the mysterious providence of God present in the life of another man, not to object that its unspoken depth and direction are something to which he has no access. The life of that disciple is hidden. So hidden that Colossians can rephrase and explain the response of Jesus: "Set your minds on things that are above, not on things that are on earth. For you have died, and your life is hid with Christ in God" (Col. 3:2–3).

As is classically noted in Catholic theology, the lives of human beings are hidden from one another, in great part also from themselves—hidden with Christ—hidden in God. The more that human beings come to know each other, the more they must bow before the mysterious providence in which each of them is held, their solitude. We know very little, so very little—how each of us was chosen by God, how the great promises of Ephesians have been or are to be realized in what we are. For our lives are defined,

3. Raymond Brown, SS, *The Gospel according to John: XIII–XXI*, Anchor Bible (New Haven: Yale University Press, 1970), 1122.

given their meaning from their direction toward God, their purpose—and this God to whom we are directed and by whom we are
specified is incomprehensible, infinitely beyond the grasp of what
we know and understand. This does not mean that we do not know
God, but that we know him precisely as inexhaustibly intelligible.
There is a mystery about human beings because human beings are
defined by God's incomprehensibility, that is, by God as mystery.

To pretend to an adequate knowledge of God, to pretend that
we are competent to judge one another, to appoint ourselves as
guardians or admonitors of one another as if we saw or understood
or even were charged with the other's destiny—is pretentious and
ludicrously ill advised. It is to erode the religious mystery of another—in an effort to lodge the other within our putative comprehensive grasp of all things. Both of these desires are illusions. To
be a Christian is to give oneself over to the unmanageable mystery
God revealed in Jesus, to the individual providence and care that
he embodies. This providence is the mystery that encloses every
life that seems so ordinary, yet one that is caught up in the unspeakable mystery of the Spirit of Christ. And that mystery allows
itself to come into the lives of others through the reverence in
which it is held. In light of these considerations, the question of
Jesus to Peter is stark.

"If I wish that he remain"—what is Jesus saying? The destiny of
John is according to the wishes of Jesus—with all the darkness and
opaqueness that hover over that destiny. A particular providence
governs the days and years that make up his life. How wisely Søren
Kierkegaard wrote of the hiddenness of such a life, one given over
to the power of God, and so beyond the comprehension of human
beings around him: "The course of development of the religious
subject has the remarkable trait that it comes into being for the
individual and closes up behind him."[4]

---

4. Søren Kierkegaard, *Concluding Unscientific Postscript*, trans. David F.
Swenson (Princeton: Princeton University Press, 1941), 62.

You know what is to come because it has already come. A mute incomprehension necessarily then obscures while it directs the life of every person. If this has failed to make itself felt, attended to, and wondered at, then one has failed to discern the person. Is this not even more true in the lives of those who have given themselves over to God, the mystery of whose lives bespeaks their specification by the mysterious God? It is this God who defines their lives, not the calculation of the thousand factors that enter into it. This is what it means to say that their life is hidden with Christ. All human beings must be reminded over and over again of the mystery that is here—within the ordinary, the very ordinary and limited.

All human beings who treat with God must encounter the danger that they will think, like Peter, that their own interests and competencies should determine the destiny of others. Under such profound disorder, albeit hidden, these persons they encounter cease to be unique subjects with a unique providence and a wondrous destiny and become *objects* instead. Such "objectification" takes the measure of those around them. It sees and evaluates their accomplishments and their failures, their moments of virtue and the embarrassing petty events that mar their lives. In a world of objects, intelligibility and vision are reduced to observation and common sense.

And where we cannot figure it out, we probe. Even with ourselves, we repeat the question of Peter: "Lord, what about this man?" What about him? What about me? What about them, the countless number of them in my life? How do these years add up, what do they mean now, what will they come to mean? How can we figure it all out? To us also, about our own lives and about the lives of those around us, comes back the question of Jesus: "What is it to you? You follow me."

If we take that last question seriously, we will admittedly never plumb the hidden depths of another human being—but we shall do something far more important. We shall come to recognize and reverence God within every person—the incomprehensible, providential God.

SCRIPTURE INDEX